Teaching Actively

Eight Steps and 32 Strategies to Spark Learning in Any Classroom

MEL SILBERMAN
Temple University

Boston   New York   San Francisco   Mexico City   Montreal   Toronto
London   Madrid   Munich   Paris   Hong Kong   Singapore   Tokyo
Cape Town   Sydney

Executive Editor and Publisher: Stephen D. Dragin
Editorial Assistant: Meaghan Minnick
Marketing Manager: Tara Kelly
Production Editor: Greg Erb
Editorial Production Service: Publishers' Design and Production Services, Inc.
Composition and Manufacturing Buyer: Andrew Turso
Electronic Composition: Publishers' Design and Production Services, Inc.
Interior Design: Publishers' Design and Production Services, Inc.
Cover Designer: Linda Knowles

For related titles and support materials, visit our online catalog at www.ablongman.com.

Between the time website information is gathered and then published, it is not unusual for some sites to have closed. Also, the transcription of URLs can result in typographical errors. The publisher would appreciate notification where these errors occur so that they may be corrected in subsequent editions.

Library of Congress Cataloging-in-Publication Data
Silberman, Melvin L.
    Teaching actively : eight steps and 32 strategies to spark learning in any classroom / Mel Silberman.
        p. cm.
    Includes bibliographical references and index.
    ISBN 0-205-45537-9 (alk. paper)
    1. Active learning. 2. Effective teaching. I. Title.

LB1027.23.S56 2006
371.102—dc22   2005047602

Printed in the United States of America

10   9   8   7   6   5   4   3   VHG   09   08   07

Contents

STEP EIGHT: Make the End Unforgettable   123

Preface

It's not what you tell your students that counts. What counts is what they take away from the classroom. That's because the more you tell them the more they will forget. You can't learn for them; they must do it themselves. Your role, therefore, is to spark and guide their learning. How to accomplish this is what Teaching Actively is all about.

Teaching Actively is a companion to the best-selling book *Active Learning: 101 Strategies to Teach Any Subject. Active Learning* is the ultimate book of recipes for teachers. It not only contains 101 ways of hosting a learning feast but includes over 100 quick tips for organizing and facilitating it. It's a book to peruse, looking for instant ideas for promoting active learning in your classroom. *Teaching Actively* is not simply a recipe book. Its objective is to guide you to be an exceptional chef who prepares meals of learning in which students will be hungry to participate. Although it's a book you don't need to read from cover to cover, it has a comprehensive plan you can follow rather than a collection of ideas from which you pick and choose.

The eight-step plan in *Teaching Actively* is for any teacher who has students with basic skills in "reading, writing, and arithmetic" and some maturity to collaborate with fellow classmates (if shown how). That may include students in upper elementary grades, middle and high schools, and institutions of higher learning. It also may include adults who participate in GED classes, welfare-to-work programs, and workplace training. I realize that this intended audience is vast and varied. Certainly, the ways in which you as a teacher relate and appeal to 10-year-olds is different from the approaches you take with adolescents, college students, and adults. However, *Teaching Actively* contains advice, suggestions, and examples that I have successfully shared with teachers at each of these levels, both in North America and throughout the world. I am confident you will find value in this book at whatever level you teach.

The Eight-Step Plan

If you want to spark active learning in your classroom, there are eight steps that will bring you success. You don't need to heed all eight steps, but most of them are critical for any teacher, at any level, and in any subject matter.

STEP ONE: ENGAGE YOUR STUDENTS FROM THE START.

Use opening activities at the beginning of a course and at the beginning of each class session to develop a climate for active learning, to promote peer interaction, and to build immediate involvement in the learning topic.

STEP TWO: BE A BRAIN-FRIENDLY TEACHER.

Present information and concepts that maximize student understanding and retention through techniques that stimulate students' brains to be mentally alert and receptive to new data.

STEP THREE: ENCOURAGE LIVELY AND FOCUSED DISCUSSION.

Structure discussion so that students are motivated to participate and pursue the topic in depth.

STEP FOUR: URGE STUDENTS TO ASK QUESTIONS.

Motivate students to ask thoughtful questions and seek information that will answer them.

STEP FIVE: LET YOUR STUDENTS LEARN FROM EACH OTHER.

Set up effective group learning and peer teaching activities that require student collaboration.

STEP SIX: ENHANCE LEARNING WITH EXPERIENCING AND DOING.

Design and facilitate games, practice exercises, role-plays, and other experiential activities that enhance the learning of information, skills, and values.

STEP SEVEN: BLEND IN TECHNOLOGY WISELY.

Effectively integrate computer-based tools such as multimedia presentation, tutorials, chat rooms, and web searches to supplement classroom learning activity.

STEP EIGHT: MAKE THE END UNFORGETTABLE.

Close a learning experience so that students review what they have learned, reflect on its importance, consider future steps, and celebrate their accomplishments.

Teaching Actively is organized around each of these eight teaching steps. Following a brief introduction about each step, you will find a group of three to five strategies that foster its implementation. Each of these strategies contains specific suggestions. A worksheet is provided for each strategy to make it easier for you to apply it to your classroom.

I hope you find *Teaching Actively* to be an eminently practical guide that will spark learning in your classroom.

About the Author

Dr. Mel Silberman is Professor Emeritus of Psychological Studies in Education at Temple University, where he won its Great Teacher Award. He has an international reputation in the field of active learning. He is the author of several books on education and training, including:

101 Ways to Make Training Active, Second Edition (Pfeiffer, 2005)

Working PeopleSmart (Berrett-Koehler, 2004)

The Best of Active Training (Pfeiffer, 2004)

The Consultant's Tool Kit (McGraw-Hill, 2001)

PeopleSmart (Berrett-Koehler, 2000)

101 Ways to Make Meetings Active (Jossey-Bass, 1999)

Active Training, Second Edition (Jossey-Bass, 1998)

Active Learning: 101 Strategies to Teach Any Subject (Allyn & Bacon, 1996)

When Your Child Is Difficult (Research Press, 1995)

Confident Parenting (Warner Books, 1988)

How to Discipline without Feeling Guilty (Dutton, 1980)

Real Learning (Little, Brown, 1976)

Under the auspices of Active Training in Princeton, New Jersey (*www.activetraining.com*; 800-924-8157), Dr. Silberman has conducted active learning seminars for pre-service and in-service teachers, adult educators, college instructors, and workplace trainers in hundreds of educational, governmental, human service, and business organizations. Dr. Silberman is a graduate of Brandeis University and holds a Ph.D. in educational psychology from The University of Chicago.

Acknowledgments

Teaching is my passion. For over 35 years I have been eagerly experimenting with ways to enliven learning for my students and sharing the results of this experimentation with other teachers. During this time, I have been blessed with many opportunities to create, refine, and test the strategies in *Teaching Actively*. Sometimes, what I've done has bombed or been met with great skepticism. I appreciate all those who helped me through the "school of hard knocks." Other times, I have been successful in sparking learning in challenging waters. I am also grateful for all the votes of confidence I've received from students and workshop participants who have welcomed my active learning approach.

No one creates in a vacuum. I have numerous mentors and colleagues who have given me more creative ideas than one mind can process. Some of the people who have shared their wisdom with me include Sharon Bowman, Maryellen Weimer, Dave Meier, Rod Napier, Karen Lawson, Sivasailam Thiagarajan, Howard Kirschenbaum, Jerry Allender, Catherine Schifter, and Susan Wheelan. I also benefited from the sound feedback of my wife, Shoshana Silberman, a talented educator who uses my techniques, extends their range, and improves upon them.

My family is a special source of joy, love, and support. Shmuel, Lisa, and Gabe, my children; son-in-law Daniel; and daughter-in-law Sara have been steadfast boosters of my passion for teaching. My grandchildren—Noam, Jonah, Yaakov, Adira, and Meir—make it all worthwhile.

Engage Your Students from the Start

To learn something well, your students need to listen, observe, ask questions, and discuss the material with others. Most important is the fact that students need to *do*. This includes figuring out things by themselves, coming up with examples, and performing tasks that depend on the knowledge they already have.

The success of active learning depends on your ability to form and sustain a classroom environment in which students take on the responsibility to be doers. Above all, students must be willing to use their brains—studying ideas, solving problems, and applying what they learn. Although many of the strategies in *Teaching Actively* are fast paced, fun, supportive, and personally engaging, you cannot depend on a grab bag of teaching tricks. There must be a learning climate right from the beginning that supports your creative methods. The longer you wait to create this climate, the longer your students will have to settle into being passive learners. Engaging students from the get-go applies to the first day of class. If you want your students to start learning actively, give them a taste of it right away. What better time to signal them that you want their brains working, their hands waving, and their mouths (and even their entire bodies) moving! However, don't relegate this practice to opening day. Treat the beginning of every class session the same way. Get your students to do something before you even start teaching. Think of it as the appetizer before the main course. Whet their appetites and they will be hungry learners. So, let's get started figuring out how to get your students active from the start.

STRATEGY #1:
Weave Course Content into Your Icebreakers
··

It's always a good idea to use the first class as a time to get to know your students and for your students to get to know one another. By doing so, you begin to create the interactive community that sustains active learning. The sections that follow explore ways of accomplishing this.

1. STRUCTURE THE INITIAL SOCIAL INTERACTIONS BETWEEN STUDENTS.

There are hundreds, perhaps even thousands, of social icebreakers that educators have invented. (My own book, *Active Learning: 101 Strategies to Teach Any Subject,* has twenty-three of them!) They tend to be fun, fast-paced ways of structuring social interaction so that even the shiest students don't need much courage to participate. The techniques employed in these activities include the following.

- Polling or voting
- Conversing in small groups or pairs
- Playing a game
- Mingling in an open space
- Obtaining very brief verbal responses
- Drawing
- Singing
- Movement

A good case in point is an activity titled the Human Scavenger Hunt. This is a popular icebreaker that can be designed in a number of ways and for any size of class. It works for children, teens, and adults alike, in that it fosters social interaction and uses physical movement at the very beginning of a class.

The process of the activity is to devise six to ten descriptive statements to complete the phrase "Find someone who . . . ." Statements typically refer to personal information, as in the following completion. Find someone who

- Has the same first initial as yours
- Likes/enjoys (reading mysteries, hip-hop music, crossword puzzles, and so on)

- Has (a pet, a tattoo, a birthday this month, etc.)
- Is motivated by (a special friend, a good preacher, money, etc.)
- Dislikes (exercise, eating breakfast, clutter, etc.)
- Owns a (laptop, skateboard, transformer, etc.) or
- Has already (been to our new library, had calculus, dozed off today, etc.)

Human Scavenger Hunt

The human scavenger items are given to students with the following instructions: "This activity is like a scavenger hunt, except that you are looking for people instead of objects. When I say 'begin,' circulate around the room looking for people who match these statements. You can use each person for only one statement, even if he or she matches more than one. When you have found a match, write down the person's first name." When most students have finished, the teacher calls a stop to the hunt and reconvenes the full class. A token prize can be given to the person who finishes first, but more importantly the teacher surveys the entire group about each of the items. (For example, the teacher can go through the alphabet and ask all those whose first name begins with A, B, C, and so forth to raise their hands and introduce themselves to the class.)

2. GO BEYOND SIMPLY ACQUAINTING STUDENTS WITH ONE ANOTHER.

Past coursework, placements, volunteering, jobs

There is no law that limits a social icebreaker to "social" information. Here is an excellent opportunity to engage students in the class content from the start. For example, an item in the Human Scavenger Hunt might require finding someone who knows a fact or concept from the subject matter you teach. You might ask the class to find someone who knows what makes Mars a place that sustains life, the capital of Wyoming, or one way to limit a web search. You might also ask who has recently read a book about _____, has had previous course work in _____, or has a great idea for _____.

Stand Up & Be Counted
• Survey
• Question applies, stand up

Another example of a social icebreaker that can go beyond personal information is one titled Stand Up and Be Counted. The process involves explaining to students that you would like to conduct a quick survey to help everyone know "who's here." The teacher asks students to *stand up and be counted* if something that is said applies to them. For example, the following are statements that relate to personal information.

Stand up if you:

- Drink milk every day
- Have more than three siblings
- Have met someone famous
- Root for the _____ [supply name of team]
- Love chocolate
- Are left-handed

Added to this mix (or replacing the items entirely so that they only refer to the subject matter) might include one of the following. Stand up if you:

- Have used a Bunsen burner
- Believe that capital punishment does not deter first degree murder
- Think your writing skills need to be improved
- Prefer sociology over psychology
- Can create a spreadsheet
- Know when to use *it's* versus *its*

So, think about the social icebreakers you already use or those you might use in the future. Don't limit them merely to "getting to know you." Introduce your subject matter within these openers. As you do that, you will advertise some of the elements of your upcoming classes, help students to become familiar with some key items, and hopefully build interest in what's to follow.

Extend activity to their classroom.

PLANNING SHEET

Weave Course Content into Your Icebreakers

Use the following sheet to implement this strategy.

Technique (check one or more):

_____ Structure the initial social interactions among students.

_____ Go beyond simply acquainting students with one another.

My Plan:

_____

_____

_____

_____

_____

_____

_____

_____

_____

_____

_____

_____

_____

_____

_____

_____

_____

_____

_____

_____

STRATEGY #2:
Create Icebreakers That Focus Solely on Immediate Learning Involvement

....

In addition to social icebreakers, consider using "learning" icebreakers. Learning icebreakers ask students to (1) respond to initial questions about the class content, (2) try out learning activities related to the subject matter without previous instruction, or (3) view presentations or demonstrations that give an initial description of knowledge and skills to be learned later on. These activities help to introduce a class in a dramatic, active manner that draws students into the class from the beginning.

1. QUIZ YOUR STUDENTS (FOR THE FUN OF IT).

Normally, quizzes are something students hate. However, a quiz can be used to form a learning icebreaker. An example is a technique titled
✳ Active Knowledge Sharing. It would work with any group and with any topic. The following outlines how this works.

Achve K Sharing

a. Devise a list of questions pertaining to the subject matter you will be teaching. You could include some or all of the following categories.

- Words to define (e.g., "What is an allegory?")
- Multiple choice questions concerning facts, concepts, procedures, and so on (e.g., you might ask, "A psychological test is valid if it (a) measures an attribute over time, or (b) measures what it purports to measure.")
- People (important to the subject matter) to identify (e.g., "Who is Leonardo da Vinci?")
- Questions concerning actions one could take in certain situations (e.g., "How do you ask a person to listen carefully to what you are about to tell them?")
- Incomplete sentences (e.g., "A _____ is a plant that requires very little water.")

b. Ask students to answer the questions as well as they can.

mill around room work together

✳ **c.** Invite students to mill around the room, finding others who can answer questions they don't know how to answer. Encourage students to help each other, or invite students to compare answers with a partner or small group of peers.

d. Reconvene the full group and review the answers. Fill in answers that are unknown to any of the students.

2. CREATE A TRUE/FALSE GAME.

Another learning icebreaker can be formed around a game titled True or False. Create an equal number of true statements and false statements about your subject matter. Assume that your students don't know the answers to many, if not most, of the statements. Place students in small groups or pairs and invite them to guess which statements (listed on a sheet of paper or displayed on a board or screen) are correct and which are incorrect. This is an effective way of causing them to become curious about what they will learn, without any stigma when they do not know the answers. The following are four true/false statements taken from a True or False icebreaker that contained a total of twelve statements.

- "Out, damned spot!" is a sentence from Shakespeare's *Othello*. (False; answer: *Macbeth*)
- *Beowolf* is the earliest long work of literature recorded in the English language. (True)
- "A rose is a rose is a rose is a rose" is a famous line from the poetry of Shelley. (False; answer: Gertrude Stein)
- *The Scarlet Letter* is a novel by Nathaniel Hawthorne. (True)

3. HAVE STUDENTS DO SOMETHING THEY'VE NEVER DONE BEFORE. *Think out of the box.*

A different way of creating learning icebreakers is to ask students to try out a skill before they are taught how to do it. At first, this idea might sound bizarre. Wouldn't students be embarrassed or angry? If a playful mood is created, however, trying to do something you are not sure how to do can be not only fun but motivating. For example, you might ask students to attempt such things as the following.

- Solve a math puzzle.
- Write a poem.
- Play a musical instrument.
- Perform a scientific experiment.
- Analyze a case study.
- Speak in a foreign language (with a lot of hand motions!).
- Draw a self-portrait. *As a teacher?*

There is no limit to the ways in which you can create a learning icebreaker. Experiment. Think "out of the box." Once you come up with a winner, you can use it year after year.

PLANNING SHEET

Create Icebreakers That Focus Solely on Immediate Learning Involvement

Use the following sheet to implement this strategy.

Technique (check one or more):

_____ Quiz your students (for the fun of it).

_____ Create a true/false game.

_____ Have students do something they've never done before.

My Plan:

_____

_____

_____

_____

_____

_____

_____

_____

_____

_____

_____

_____

_____

_____

_____

_____

_____

_____

STRATEGY #3:
Give Students Something to Do before
Each Class Session Formally Starts

make this practice before each class

You are well into the course. Your students are gathering for the next lesson, unit, or class session. Most teachers wait until they have everyone's attention and then launch into their lesson. Why not give your students something, on topic, to do before you call the class to order? That action will get their brains active in the same way race car drivers are motivated when they hear "Start your engines!" Better yet, make this your practice before every class. Your students will come to class wondering what you've dreamed up next for them to do. Let's explore some options that give students something to do before you teach.

1. DISPLAY A QUESTION IN FULL VIEW OF GATHERING STUDENTS.

As students enter the classroom, display, for example, one of the following.

- A quotation to interpret (e.g., What does this mean?: "A penny saved is a penny earned.")
- A provocative question to answer (e.g., What makes a body in space a planet?)
- An interesting problem to solve (e.g., Find three numbers such that each of them is a square of the difference of the two others)

Give students a few minutes to work individually or in pairs.

2. HAND OUT A PRE-CLASS ACTIVITY.

Hand out to students a sheet of paper containing a pre-class activity that involves words, problems, graphics, or other connections to the material you are about to teach. Such activities include the following.

- A brief crossword puzzle
- Scrambled words
- A word search
- A document riddled with errors
- A math problem

- A list of vocabulary words to define or translate
- A short, fun multiple-choice quiz
- An interesting survey to complete
- A story that needs an ending

3. ASK STUDENTS TO CREATE A QUESTION.

Give students an index card as they await the lesson and invite them to write down a question they might have about the upcoming topic. They can write a question alone or together with a student partner. The question might fall into the following areas.

- The content of a reading assignment (e.g., "Does the *Merchant of Venice* prove that Shakespeare was anti-Semitic?")
- Homework that was given (e.g., "What's the answer to the third math problem you gave us?")
- Something of curiosity to the student about the topic to follow (e.g., "Where does electricity come from?")

You can collect the question cards and read as many as you can before you begin. You can also shuffle the cards and redistribute them so that each student receives someone else's question. Then, you can invite willing students to read the question on their card and ask you to answer it or attempt to answer it by themselves.

PLANNING SHEET

Give Students Something to Do before Each Class Session Formally Starts

Use the following sheet to implement this strategy.

Technique (check one or more):

_____ Display a question in full view of gathering students.

_____ Hand out a pre-class activity.

_____ Ask students to create a question.

My Plan:

_____

_____

_____

_____

_____

_____

_____

_____

_____

_____

_____

_____

_____

_____

_____

_____

_____

STRATEGY #4:
Enlarge the Pool of Participation at the Very Beginning

Beyond any structured activities, your classroom will not spark active learning unless students are eager to participate. The bad news is that only a small minority will actively participate (raise their hands, volunteer, ask questions, and so forth) throughout the semester or school year unless you do something to increase the number of participants right from the start. Once the frequent participators are established (often, it's no more than four students), it's very difficult to increase the pool of participation.

Many teachers assume that several students do not participate because they are either shy, academically insecure, or disinterested. Of course, that's true for some students but hardly for the majority. Rates of participation are much more influenced by the teacher than determined by the students. I have observed time and again that many teachers have a habit they are unaware of. This habit leads to lower participation and needs to be changed. Are you curious what habit I'm referring to?

Assuming the teacher asks interesting questions, sets a nonthreatening climate, and encourages student response, the one problematic behavior I often see is that teachers *call on the first student whose hand is raised*. The reason this occurs is that it seems rude not to do so, especially if the student in question does not volunteer constantly. In addition, many teachers are grateful that the student is raising his or her hand when the rest of the class seems disinterested or afraid. The problem that arises is that students (and teachers) get used to only a single volunteer (or maybe just a few) and the pattern and rate of participation becomes fixed. Sooner or later, a small minority of students fill the role of responding to teacher requests for participation.

Without realizing it, most teachers even use language that promotes a small pool of responsive students. They say things such as "*Who* wants to read next?" "Can *anyone* tell me what's the solution here?" and "I'm looking for *someone* to. . . ."

The following are five guaranteed ways to increase the pool of participation. You don't need to do all of them, but you should get in the habit, as soon as possible, of employing some of them. Also, don't expect great results the very first time you use the techniques you select. The good news is that once the students get the hang of what you are doing, even after one exposure, they will start to respond with greater frequency.

5 ways ↑ participation

1. CREATE THE OPPORTUNITY FOR PRE-DISCUSSION.

Think, Pair, Share

- Pose a question and invite students to discuss it with someone seated next to them.
- Next, ask the question again for a total group discussion.

2. OBTAIN A COMMITMENT TO PARTICIPATE.

- Pose a question and ask "How many of you have some thoughts about this?"
- Encourage several students to raise their hands before you call on any student.
- Call on students who have not participated so far, or if time is available call on all hands raised.

3. SPECIFY HOW MANY YOU WISH TO PARTICIPATE.

- Ask a question and open it up to the entire group.
- Say "I'd like to ask four or five students to give me their opinions."

4. ESTABLISH A "NEW" PARTICIPANT RULE.

- Pose a question.
- Say "I'd like a new participant this time. Who hasn't contributed yet?"

5. USE THE "CALL ON THE NEXT SPEAKER" FORMAT.

- Ask students to raise their hands when they want to share their views, and request that the present speaker in the class call on the next speaker (rather than the teacher performing this role).
- Say "When you are the speaker, please talk to your classmates rather than addressing me."

PLANNING SHEET

Enlarge the Pool of Participation at the Very Beginning

Use the following sheet to implement this strategy.

Technique (check one or more):

_____ Create the opportunity for "pre-discussion."

_____ Obtain a commitment to participate.

_____ Specify how many you wish to participate.

_____ Establish a "new" participant rule.

_____ Use the "call on the next speaker" format.

My Plan:

_____

_____

_____

_____

_____

_____

_____

_____

_____

_____

_____

_____

_____

_____

_____

_____

_____

_____

Be a Brain-Friendly Teacher

Your students' brains are your best allies. Too often, teachers think that there is nothing going on in their students' heads. Nothing could be further from the truth. Technically speaking, if nothing is happening in students' brains they are *dead*. Their brains are *alive* and working (even when they are asleep). The issue is what are their brains thinking about?

I appreciate the fear that students are thinking about everything but what you want them to focus on. Yes, students, like all human beings, do a lot of "mind-surfing." Your task is twofold: to interest their brains in what you are teaching and to help their brains to really go to work so that they learn and retain the lesson.

Before presenting some strategies on how to get their brains on your side, let's back up a moment and examine further why you need to be a brain-friendly teacher. The brain does not function like an audiotape or videotape recorder. Because of its storehouse of prior information, incoming information is continually being questioned. The brain asks questions such as:

- Have I heard or seen this information before? What does it remind me of?
- Where does this information fit? What can I do with it?

The brain doesn't just receive information—it *processes* it. Our job, as teachers, is to facilitate that processing. In many ways, the brain can be compared to a computer. Although a computer can receive information on its own, it needs software to interpret the data. Students' brains need to engage their own software as well. Their brains need to link what they are being taught with what they already know and how they already think and learn. When students are denied that opportunity, their learning is passive and their brains don't make these connections. Furthermore, a computer cannot retain information it has processed without "saving it." Students also need to test information, recap it, or perhaps explain it to someone else in order to store information in their memory banks. When learning is passive, the brain doesn't save what has been presented. It may stay in temporary memory for a short time, but it will not make it into permanent memory.

What occurs when teachers flood students with their own thoughts (however insightful and well organized they are) or when they rely too often on "let me show you how" demonstrations and explanations? Pouring facts and concepts into students' heads and masterfully performing skills can actually interfere with student learning. The presentation may make an immediate impression on the brain, but it may lull students into thinking they will never forget what they heard and saw. However, students simply cannot retain very much for any period of time unless they do the work to store information intelligently. That work can't be done solely by the teacher, regardless of how dynamic he or she is.

The bottom line is that just because you "covered" certain information with your students does not mean that it was "uncovered" by them. Fortunately, there are a number of brain-friendly ways to teach information, concepts, and skills that maximize student understanding and retention. Let's take a look.

STRATEGY #5:
Build Brain Interest in What Is Being Taught
....

The first brain-friendly strategy to consider if you want learning to occur is to get into your students' heads. Using the computer metaphor, you want them to bring your material onto their "desktops" rather than something else that will distract them from the lesson at hand. That way, the information coming into their brains is your information rather than other miscellaneous data. Instead of diving right into your content, try building your students' *brain interest and involvement* in the subject matter. Consider the four techniques discussed in the following sections (with examples) in trying to do just that.

1. LEAD OFF THE LESSON WITH A STORY OR INTERESTING VISUAL.

To build interest right away, a story or a dramatic visual might grab your students' attention. The following are some examples.

- Show slides that startle students (e.g., a past and current map of farm land demonstrating drastic change).
- Tell true stories with unusual events or surprise endings (e.g., an account of the Bay of Pigs fiasco in Cuba back in the early part of John F. Kennedy's brief term as president).
- Present an object that students may never have seen or touched before (e.g., the insides of a frog).
- Read a fable, allegory, or fictional letter that makes a dramatic point (e.g., Hans Christian Andersen's *The Emperor's New Suit*).
- Display a chart containing interesting numerical data (e.g., a series of numbers that all have even square roots).

After presenting the story or visual, make the connection to today's lesson or challenge students to discover it. For example, a psychology teacher is about to lecture on the validity of IQ tests. Before the start of her lesson, she displays a list of the vocabulary words on the Wechsler Intelligence Scale for Children. She then asks students if they thought the use of such vocabulary words is a valid way of testing intelligence. After receiving a variety of opinions (mostly dissenting), she proceeds to explain how IQ test developers defend the use of vocabulary words in testing intelligence.

2. PRESENT A SHORT PROBLEM.

You can also build interest by structuring a lesson around a problem. The following are some examples.

- An account of a mathematician who wants to solve an equation he's never been able to solve before
- A case study in which an editor must reduce a 60-word paragraph to a 35-word paragraph without altering the information it provides
- A document written in French that needs to be translated so that someone can claim an inheritance
- A detective story that requires scientific knowledge to solve the crime

The following is a case-study problem used to introduce a lesson on résumé writing.

Joan has been an employee of a national pharmaceutical company for the last seven years. She began her work at the company as a secretary in the human resources department, and after four years moved into an entry-level position as a benefits administrator. Her job responsibilities included answering employees' benefit questions, handling the enrollment of new employees into one of the company's medical plans, and researching any problems employees had as they filed insurance claims with the medical plan providers.

Yesterday, Joan found out that her job had been eliminated. All responsibility for benefits administration will now be handled out of corporate headquarters in New York. Joan and three other coworkers have been told that they will be let go at the end of the month. Once having left the company, each will receive three months of job severance pay.

Joan is terrified of looking for a new job. She enjoyed working at the company very much, and hates to think of starting all over again somewhere else. Moreover, she has not written a résumé since the last time she had to look for a new job. The old résumé identified only her skills as a secretary, yet Joan is certain she would like to continue her career in benefits and not return to a secretarial position.

What advice could you give Joan as she writes her new résumé? As I present some tips on résumé writing, think through how Joan can best present her last seven years of work at the pharmaceutical company. I'll ask you for your ideas when I'm done.

3. ASK AN OPENING QUESTION.

A question related to the lesson topic might motivate students to engage their brains. Pose a question to your students and encourage them to give the best answer they can. Even invite them to make a guess when the question is beyond their knowledge. Don't tell them if they are right or wrong. Merely thank them and ask: "Would you like to know the answer?" Promise them that you will explain the answer during the lesson. The following are some questions that might get them curious.

- Why do we need geographers?
- What is cancer?
- What is infinity?
- What do you think Shakespeare's play *Much Ado about Nothing* is about? About what might people make "much ado"?
- How does a tornado happen?
- How can the stock market do well during a period of inflation?

4. GIVE HIGHLIGHTS OR "COMING ATTRACTIONS" OF THE LESSON.

With enthusiasm, tell your students what's to follow. Focus both on the features (what will happen) and benefits (what students will take away) of the lesson. The following are some examples.

- "Today, we will look at how to conduct an effective job search, including how to network and how to use the Internet. I hope you will get some tips you can use right away."
- "We are going to compare the poetry of Robert Frost to that of e. e. cummings. We will take a look at Frost's poem 'The Road Not Taken' and at cummings' poem 'if I love You.' Let's see which one you end up liking more."
- "The next thing we will learn is how to multiply whole numbers and decimals. For example, I will show you how to multiply 145 by .25. One of the things you can do with this skill is figure out how much you will pay for something on sale when you don't know the sale price but do know you're getting 25 percent off."

PLANNING SHEET

Build Brain Interest in What Is Being Taught

Use the following sheet to implement this strategy.

Technique (check one or more):

_____ Lead off with a story or interesting visual.

_____ Present a short problem.

_____ Ask an opening question.

_____ Give highlights of "coming attractions" of the lesson.

My Plan:

_____

_____

_____

_____

_____

_____

_____

_____

_____

_____

_____

_____

_____

_____

_____

_____

_____

_____

STRATEGY #6:
Help Your Students' Brains to "Get It"

After engaging the interest of your students, it is time to begin the actual lesson. As you put it together, remember that your goal is to maximize your students' understanding and retention of the subject matter. Don't assume, however, that they will "get it"—let alone remember it—even if you explain the material clearly. Consider the five techniques discussed in the following sections (with examples) in trying to do just that.

1. PRESENT YOUR MAJOR POINTS AND CONCLUSIONS UP FRONT.

Note how the following opening remarks provide advance notice of what's to follow and help to organize students' listening.

A high school teacher is about to talk about business writing styles. He says: "To achieve an appropriate style for a specific writing occasion in business, you must speak to the reader in an appropriate way. It is particularly important to present that information in a way that helps readers more readily understand what you have to say. Most important to least important order is preferred by most business readers and writers because it is easy to read. The most important points are clearly stated at the beginning, and less important evidence or arguments are relegated to minor positions in the body of the piece. I'm going to show you how this works in summaries, memoranda, and letters requesting information."

The following is another example.

A science teacher began a presentation on Earth visits to Mars with the following opening summary: "Mars passed closer to Earth this past summer than it had in thousands of years, and now three emissaries from Earth are set to descend on the planet and stay. Up till now, landing on Mars has been very hard. Two-thirds of all flights to Mars have failed. I will tell you about previous attempts by Russia, Japan, and the United States and what problems occurred. We will also look at the three missions to come. If they succeed, their investigations are expected to test the hypothesis that Mars was once a much more dynamic planet, warmer and wetter, and therefore supported some living organisms."

2. REDUCE THE MAJOR POINTS IN THE LESSON TO BULLETED POINTS.

Bulleted points act as headlines or memory aids. Display these bullets as you present your material in more detail. The following are some further suggestions.

- The shorter the bulleted text the better. You might even go for a single word. For example, a lesson on the Heimlich maneuver might be developed around three simple words: *encircle, lock,* and *squeeze.*

- Grab interest by making each point sound like a newspaper headline or TV ad. For example, "Different Strokes for Different Folks" might be an attention-getting headline when you want to explain how people are motivated in different ways.

- Don't always explain the bulleted point yourself. Invite students to guess its meaning. For example, you might ask students to have a brief discussion with a partner on the meaning of an item that states "Stress can be good for you."

- Use a mnemonic device by composing your major points into an acronym (the first letters of the points or facts taken together form a word). For example, the following is a **PROPOSAL** for listening effectively.

  P   *Probe for understanding.*

  R   *Reflect back to the speaker what you have heard.*

  O   *One thing at a time (listen only; don't do anything else).*

  P   *Pause before responding.*

  O   *Observe what's not being said.*

  S   *Summarize what the speaker has told you.*

  A   *Acknowledge what the speaker is saying.*

  L   *Let the speaker finish.*

3. PROVIDE USER-FRIENDLY EXAMPLES.

Today's students usually learn better from concrete examples than from abstract definitions. Furthermore, many students learn inductively more easily than deductively. For example, if you were discussing the natural resources of a region or state, giving concrete examples students understand will help them induce the concept faster than deducing the concept from examples given after an abstract example. The following are some tips when selecting user-friendly examples.

- Think about daily activities everyone experiences (e.g., taking a short shower conserves more water and electricity/gas than a long shower).
- Allude to the TV programs your students watch, products they buy, social activities they enjoy, and musical preferences they have (e.g., hip-hop is an example of music that breaks the rules in the same way as atonal music did in the early twentieth century).
- Mention well-known people who illustrate certain traits or actions (e.g., Dr. Martin Luther King Jr. is a perfect example of a "moral leader").
- Create interesting stories or case histories that contain examples of your subject matter (e.g., the story of the invasion of Iraq in 2003 contains many examples of foreign policy concepts such as "pre-emptive war" and "unilateralism").

The following is how by opening a unit on "Alcoholism and the Family" with a gripping example a psychology teacher explains how family members may not be the cause of a parent's alcoholism but may play a role in keeping the problem alive.

Consider the family of George, a retired mechanical engineer and an alcoholic. George began as a social drinker and eventually stepped over the invisible line into alcoholism. His wife, Joann, a registered nurse, played a key role in enabling George to remain an alcoholic. By taking on many of George's responsibilities, including budgeting, providing additional income, and handling the physical maintenance of the home, Joann was able to ensure that the household ran smoothly. In the process, of course, George did not have to confront his alcoholism. George's eldest children, Bill and Cathy, also contributed to the enabling process. As successful people outside the family, both children projected appearances of "having it together," but in truth they were often depressed. A younger sister, Laura, did her share by becoming a difficult teenager, refocusing family anger away from father to her. All members of the family adopted three rules that helped maintain the status quo: (1) keep negative feelings to yourself, (2) don't talk about Dad's drinking with other family members, and (3) don't let outsiders know what happens in the family.

4. USE AN ANALOGY TO EXPLAIN YOUR MATERIAL.

Earlier, when I compared a brain to a computer, I was using an analogy to help you understand my views on being a brain-friendly teacher. When I mentioned in the introduction to this book that its purpose was to help you to become a chef preparing a learning feast, I was using a metaphor. These are not literal examples of ideas but are figurative. You can paint pictures in your students' mind in the same way. Many well-known concepts are explained effectively by way of analogy. The following are two.

- A database will hold and organize information for you like a *file cabinet*. Your information is stored in files like the *folders* in your file cabinet.
- A body's ability to contain stress is much like *a rain barrel* that overflows when the water reaches the top. We all have rain barrels for containing our stress. As they begin to fill, we start to experience stress-related symptoms. When they reach the point of overflowing, we may have serious illnesses.

To aid you in creating analogies and metaphors, consider types of comparison such as the following.

- A familiar object (e.g., a *piston* can be compared to a *cannon*)
- A popular term or expression (e.g., *redundancy* means *been there, done that*)
- An advertiser's motto (e.g., *showing initiative* means you *just do it*)
- A common experience (e.g., a *meteor shower* is like *pimples* that keep appearing)
- A physical activity (e.g., *economic stagnation* is like *running in place*)
- A song, book, or movie title (e.g., *disaster relief services* are like *building a bridge over troubled waters*)
- An animal (e.g., a bull market charges ahead, whereas a bear market goes into hibernation)

5. EMPLOY VISUALS ALONG WITH WORDS.

If your students "see" the point rather than just "hear" it, they are more likely to remember it. There are a number of ways to add visuals in your classroom, such as those that follow. Some of these can be employed on a regular basis, whereas others are for special occasions.

- *Presentation slides:* Content presented by slides can visually anchor verbal presentations. They can be enhanced with color, graphics, animation, and audio/video streaming.

- *Handwritten text and graphics:* Important issues, questions, and solutions can be recorded on chart paper or on the black/white board. Adding color and visual graphics enhances the display.

- *Objects:* You can utilize props, equipment, play gear, sculpture, machinery, or any three-dimensional materials that directly or indirectly describe key elements of your subject matter.

- *Documents:* Use reports, diagrams, charts, maps, pictures, or other similar images when they help to explain what you are presenting. It's usually better to have a copy for each participant rather than one copy that is displayed or passed around.

- *Vivid stories:* Tell stories that illustrate the points you are making. The more visual details you include in the story the more your students will be engaged.

- *Decorations:* Place colorful items in the classroom that are visually stimulating, such as art, crafts, flowers/plants, furniture, banners, balloons, and other decorative things.

- *Dramatic activity:* By asking your students to watch and/or participate in dramatizations of real work life or fictional events, they can "see" how key actions unfold.

- *Demonstration:* Show your students how something is accomplished rather than telling them verbally. Involve them, if possible, in the demonstration.

- *Simulation:* Let your students experience the nature of events, procedures, and problems on a level that approximates or symbolizes the real thing. The visual aspects of simulations are usually unforgettable.

- *Mental imagery:* Invite your students to visualize situations, both probable and improbable, by having them create mental images evoked by words.

The following is an example of using visuals effectively.

To explain how the Internet works, a teacher uses two visual illustrations. In the first illustration, the squares represent computers and the lines represent the cables that connect the computers together to form a network. If computer 1 wanted to send a message to computer 5, that message would have to pass through several cables. The Internet is a network of computers around the world that are connected in a "web" similar to that shown in the second of the following illustrations.

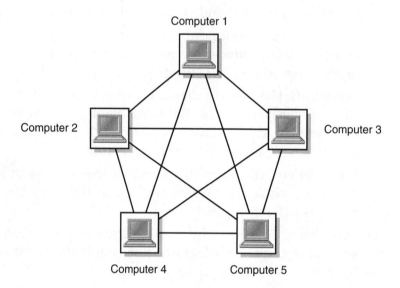

PLANNING SHEET

Help Your Students' Brains to "Get It"
Use the following sheet to implement this strategy.

Technique (check one or more):

_____ Present your major points and conclusions up front.

_____ Reduce the major points in the lesson to bulleted points.

_____ Provide user-friendly examples.

_____ Use an analogy to explain your material.

_____ Employ visuals along with words.

My Plan:

_____

_____

_____

_____

_____

_____

_____

_____

_____

_____

_____

_____

_____

_____

_____

_____

STRATEGY #7:
Involve Students Often in the Middle of Your Lesson

No matter how scintillating your presentation, your students are still placed in a passive role as they listen and watch you. Going on too long will leave many students behind unless you break up your presentation with periods of student activity. Some experts advocate that you should never exceed 10 minutes of lecture with adults before changing the action. From this advice, it follows that younger students require even shorter spans of passive listening. Fortunately, steps can be taken to enlist student participation during the middle periods of your lesson. Consider the following five techniques (with examples) in trying to do just that.

1. GIVE STUDENTS A JOB TO DO.

Assign students the responsibility of listening actively to you or of watching something so that at break points in your presentation they are able to produce points they agree or disagree with, questions toward clarifying the material, a summary of content, or quiz questions for other students. Assignments can be given to the group as a whole, to teams, or to specific individuals. The following are some examples.

- Before watching a video on global warming, students are given index cards on which to write questions they have about its content.
- As a teacher presents the Bill of Rights in the U.S. Constitution, students are asked to write down examples they might use to illustrate each right.
- A teacher is showing students how to test the acidic/alkaline balance in soil. Students are told in advance that they will be asked to explain the test to their seat partner when the teacher is finished.
- A teacher makes a case for why Stephen King is not a good writer. Students are encouraged to critique the teacher's presentation.

2. HAVE STUDENTS WRITE OR TAKE NOTES DURING THE LESSON.

Stop at intervals so that students write down information, reactions, or ideas about what you have presented. To assist your students, you might provide a preset form or work sheet for them to use that lists the major subtopics of your presentation. Leave plenty of space for note taking. The result will look something like the following.

The Food Pyramid

Use sparingly:

2–3 servings a day:

2–4 servings a day:

3–5 servings a day:

5–11 servings a day:

Alternatively, before beginning your lesson tell your students to take out a blank piece of paper and divide it into three columns. At the top of each column, ask them to draw: (1) a book (for important facts), (2) a lightbulb (for the "ahas" or "new ideas"), and (3) a question mark (for any questions they have). Stop at different times and tell students to write one word or phrase in one of the columns.

Easier yet is a form that contains what appears to be a handout, but with missing words. All students have to do is fill in the blanks. Some of the ways to do this include the following.

- Provide a series of terms and their definitions, leaving either the terms or their definitions blank.

  entropy: _____

  _____: *a period in art in which geometric shapes were common.*

- Leave one or more of a series of points blank.

  Qualifications for becoming President of the United States:

  - _____

  - _____

  - _____

  - _____

- Omit key words from a short paragraph.

  Paul _____ le fils d'un _____ de Philadelphie qui aime _____ la France, et qui a _____ que _____ fils commencent a _____ français de bonne _____.

3. KEEP STUDENTS "ON THEIR TOES" MENTALLY.

You can do this informally by asking questions, such as:

- How many of you can give me an example of _____ (e.g., an inert gas)?
- Given what you now know, how do you think the problem of _____ (e.g., homelessness) can be solved?
- Who remembers what _____ (e.g., a dangling participle) is? How do you _____ (e.g., find the lowest common denominator)?
- What do you think of _____ (e.g., this short story)?
- How would you apply this information to _____ (e.g., creating a budget)?
- What is the result of _____ (e.g., soil erosion)?
- How can you use _____ (e.g., Google)?
- What's the opposite of _____ (e.g., populism)?

You can also make a game out of keeping your students mentally alert. One example is Lesson Bingo. To utilize this technique, proceed as follows.

1. Create a lesson with up to nine key points (or identify key terms or names mentioned in your lesson).
2. Develop a bingo card that contains these key points on a 3 × 3 grid. Place a different point in each of the boxes. If you have fewer than nine key points, leave some boxes empty.
3. Create additional bingo cards with the same key points, but place the points in different boxes. The result should be that none of the bingo cards are alike in terms of where the points are located.
4. Distribute the bingo cards to your students. Also, provide them with a strip of nine self-sticking colored dots. Instruct your students that as your lesson proceeds from point to point they should place a dot on their cards for each point you discuss. (Note: Empty boxes cannot be covered with a dot.)
5. As students collect three vertical, horizontal, or diagonal dots in a row they yell "bingo!"
6. Complete the lesson. Allow students to obtain bingo as many times as they can.
7. As a variation on the previous, devise a set of questions that are answered in the lesson. Create bingo cards with the answers to these questions. Pause at different intervals in your lesson and ask only

the questions that match the information you have already presented. Have students apply a sticker on the answer they choose. State the correct answer. If any students are incorrect, they must remove the sticker before going on with the game.

A second example is Team Quiz. This technique is an enjoyable and nonthreatening way of increasing your students' accountability for what they are learning from a lesson. To utilize this technique, proceed as follows.

1. Choose a topic that can be presented in three segments.

2. Divide your students into three teams.

3. Explain the format of the lesson and start the presentation. Limit it to 10 minutes or less.

4. Have Team A prepare a short-answer quiz based on the first segment of the lesson. The quiz should take no more than five minutes to prepare. Teams B and C use this time to review their notes.

5. Team A quizzes a member of Team B. If Team B cannot answer the question, Team C gets an opportunity to answer the same question.

6. Team A directs its next question to a member of Team C and repeats the process. Team A continues asking questions until the quiz is complete.

7. When the quiz is over, continue with the second segment of your lesson, and appoint Team B as quizmaster.

8. After Team B completes its quiz, continue with the third segment of your lesson, and appoint Team C as quizmaster.

9. A different approach is to give teams prepared quiz questions from which they select when it is their turn to be the quizmaster.

10. If you want to simplify this technique, conduct one continuous lesson. Divide students into two teams. At the end of the lesson, have the two teams quiz each other.

4. ADD A BRIEF ACTIVITY THAT ILLUMINATES THE TOPIC.

One way of illuminating what you are teaching is to conduct an exercise that illustrates points you want to make. In this instance, you can use a dramatic technique such as a role-playing exercise to involve your students. For example, you might conduct a mock trial in which you debate an issue, using witnesses, prosecutors, defenders, friends of the court, and so forth. Examples of "crimes" for which someone or something might be tried follow.

- A literary character or real person with moral failings
- A controversial book or issue
- An unproven theory
- A value that does not have merit
- A faulty law

You can also employ a brief experience that simulates the real thing. For example, a health teacher wanted to illustrate how quickly HIV can spread if safe sex practices are not followed. Students were each given a blank index card. However, one student's card contained a small X in the lower right-hand corner. Students were told to mingle around the classroom and approach another student. As a result, students were now in pairs. After telling each other their names, they were asked to show their partner their index card. If the card was totally blank, the partner did not do anything to his or her card. If it contained an X, the partner had to write an X on his or her card. Students were told to keep approaching other students and showing each other their card. The same instructions were maintained. As students increased their "contact" with others, the X multiplied. After the exercise, the students could see how quickly HIV can spread from just one "carrier."

PLANNING SHEET

Involve Your Students Often in the Middle of Your Lesson
Use the following sheet to implement this strategy.

Technique (check one or more):

_____ Give students a job to do.

_____ Have students write or take notes during the lesson.

_____ Keep students "on their toes" mentally.

_____ Add a brief activity that illuminates the topic.

My Plan:

_____

_____

_____

_____

_____

_____

_____

_____

_____

_____

_____

_____

_____

_____

_____

_____

_____

STRATEGY #8:
Help Students "Save" the Lesson in Their Brains
....

When a lesson is completed, your students' brains need the opportunity to do something that starts the process of encoding the material. Once any information is recognized and attended to, it moves into *working memory*. In working memory, students do their own thinking and decide what to do with the information. If they decide that parts of it are not needed, those parts are immediately forgotten. Only what they choose to process further can be encoded into *long-term memory*.

Don't wrap up your lesson with your own summary. All that does is give students something else to listen passively to and ultimately forget. Give them something to *do* so that they review or "save" the lesson in their brains. Consider the following four methods.

1. INVITE STUDENTS TO SELECT A REVIEW QUESTION.

Provide a list of questions from which students select. For example, at the end of a lesson on electrical circuits a teacher gives students three questions that emerged from the material he had just covered. Students are asked to vote for one question to be answered by the teacher before he continues with new material. By doing this, the teacher helps his students review what he had taught.

2. ASK STUDENTS TO RECAP THE CONTENT OF THE LESSON.

The recap can be done individually, with a partner, or in a small group. A fun way to give this brief assignment is to ask students to imagine that they had to explain the lesson to someone outside the class (a friend or family member) and needed to assess themselves to see if they would be successful. Another alternative is to give your students a self-scoring review test in which you, the teacher, do not get to see the results.

3. ASK STUDENTS HOW THE LESSON APPLIES TO THEM.

Give students the chance to reflect on how they can use in their own lives the knowledge or skill you have just taught. Utilize any group format you feel will maximize the quality of the processing. For example, a teacher has just completed a lesson on good nutrition. She divides her students into trios and asks each trio to discuss the following two questions: (1) "What information was new for you and what was not?" and (2) "Which types of changes do you want to make in your eating habits?"

4. POSE A FINAL CASE-STUDY PROBLEM.

Give students a problem to solve based on the information given in the lesson. You can repeat a problem you may have used at the beginning of your lesson or give your students a brand-new problem. For example, a music teacher gives students a case-study problem in which they must convert a composition from one time signature to another. It requires the ability to apply the examples given in her lesson.

PLANNING SHEET

Help Students "Save" the Lesson in Their Brains
Use the following sheet to implement this strategy.

Technique (check one or more):

_____ Invite students to select a review question.

_____ Ask students to recap the content of the lesson.

_____ Ask students how the lesson applies to them.

_____ Pose a final case-study problem.

My Plan:

_____

_____

_____

_____

_____

_____

_____

_____

_____

_____

_____

_____

_____

_____

_____

_____

_____

Encourage Lively and Focused Discussion

Lively, focused discussions are often the best moments in a classroom. Students are engaged and time flies. All too often, however, as a teacher tries to stimulate discussion he or she is met with uncomfortable silence while students are wondering who will dare to speak up first. Sooner or later, some do. But, in your experience, how many? When I tell teachers that the average number of frequent participators in virtually every classroom is *four,* they are not surprised. The number comes close to their experience. When I tell them that they are not just any old four students but the same four students, day in and day out, they think a bit and usually agree that that's true in many of their classes as well. What is your experience?

So much for lively discussions! You just hear from the same usual suspects. Yet, there are good days and better classroom groups when the participation is greater. However, a different problem emerges. There are a lot of students participating, but the discussion goes off on tangents and/or the quality is disappointing. It may feel rewarding to have so many students involved, but is the time taken really worth it?

There are five dependable strategies you can use to obtain lively *and* focused discussions, time after time. It may help that the topic is really interesting, but these strategies bring such good results that even less-than-thrilling (but nonetheless important) topics work out fine. These strategies are certain to stimulate discussion. Some will even create heated, but manageable, exchanges between students. All of them are designed so that *many* students are involved and *several* comments are worthwhile.

STRATEGY #9:
Engage Students before Plunging into Discussion

The notion that you have to build interest first is just as true for discussions as it is for brain-friendly lessons. Merely stating a question is not usually enough to attract students. Some engagement suggestions are explored in the sections that follow.

1. SURVEY STUDENT OPINION FIRST.

Ask students one or more questions that elicit their initial opinions. The trick here is to devise polling questions that are both concrete enough and safe enough that students are willing to respond. Examples include the following.

- How many of you are in favor of _____ (e.g., all-volunteer armies)?
- Who likes _____ (e.g., alternative rock)?
- Who believes that _____ (e.g., cell phones) are good for us? bad for us?

You can add interest to the survey by obtaining responses in fun ways. For example, instead of asking students to simply raise their hands, have them raise both hands (or put "two thumbs up") if their feelings are very strong. You can also ask them to fold their arms if they are not sure of their opinion. Finally, they can put one or two "thumbs down" in disagreement.

Another technique is to ask students to move out of their seats and go to a corner of the classroom that represents their response (e.g., a "strongly agree," "agree," "disagree," and "strongly disagree" corner). A variation of this idea is to request that students take seats according to their opinion. In a large classroom, for example, students who agree with a question can get up and sit on the left-hand side of the room, whereas students who disagree can sit on the right-hand side. Students who are unsure can sit in a middle section.

2. DISTRIBUTE A COMPELLING DOCUMENT.

Find an interesting document connected to the discussion topic. Such documents might include the following.

- A newspaper or magazine article (e.g., *Brother Who Turned in the Unabomber Speaks out Against Capital Punishment*)
- A cartoon (e.g., a *Peanuts* cartoon about the dulling effects of television)
- A chart (e.g., a table that compares the energy costs of producing a paper cup and a foam cup)
- A photocopy of an object (e.g., a voter registration card)
- An image (e.g., a photo from the book *The Family of Man*)

Ask for students' overall reactions to the document or for replies to a specific question (e.g., "How many of you are surprised that paper cups, even though they are biodegradable, require more energy consumption to produce than foam cups?"). After obtaining responses, segue to your discussion topic (e.g., "Should we give up certain conveniences out of concern for the environment? If so, which ones and why?").

3. PROVIDE CONTRASTING OPINIONS ON A TOPIC.

You can accomplish this by:

- Two opposing quotations (e.g., "If it ain't broke, don't break it." versus "If it ain't broke, break it.")
- Two or more op-ed pieces or letters to the editor that contain different positions (e.g., for and against funding for space exploration)
- Interview excerpts from two or more experts or well-known personalities (e.g., two governors who take different stands on right-to-die cases)
- Video footage in conflict with one another (e.g., a cheering crowd after a military success and an angry crowd)

4. KICK OFF A DISCUSSION WITH A PANEL.

This well-known approach can vary widely in design. For example, you might assemble a group of panelists who all speak briefly and then question and debate each other. The audience can be included after a while. By contrast, you can ask a small group of students to act as panelists and then open up the discussion very quickly to the rest of the class.

PLANNING SHEET

Engage Students before Plunging into Discussion
Use the following sheet to implement this strategy.

Technique (check one or more):

_____ Survey student opinion first.

_____ Distribute a compelling document.

_____ Provide contrasting opinions on a topic.

_____ Kick off a discussion with a panel.

My Plan:

_____

_____

_____

_____

_____

_____

_____

_____

_____

_____

_____

_____

_____

_____

_____

_____

_____

STRATEGY #10:
State Effective Questions for Discussion

Merely choosing a topic and tossing it out for discussion can be a recipe for disaster. For example, take the topic of "capital punishment." If you were to ask students "Do you believe in capital punishment?" one or more of the following might occur.

- Some students won't be clear what you mean by "believe in capital punishment." Does it mean "condone," "have faith in," "agree wish," or just what?

- Some students will assume that capital punishment involves "the electric chair," whereas others will assume it involves lethal injection. The fact that there are different methods might create confusion in the discussion.

- Some students will think that you're asking if people should ever be executed for committing a murder and will cast their votes accordingly. Essentially, they will be viewing the question philosophically. Other students will interpret the question to mean "Under which circumstances do you believe in capital punishment?" and therefore not be responding to the ultimate question of whether it is ever permissible to take someone's life. As a result, two different discussions might ensue at the same time.

- Because the question is stated both very broadly and very close-ended (a yes/no question), there may be a lot of heat but little light in the discussion.

You might counter that if any of the previous problems occur a teacher can intervene and modify the course of the discussion. However, an ounce of prevention is worth a pound of cure. The way to prevent confusion is to think carefully how you want to state the discussion question. There are four things to keep in mind in this regard. These are explored in the sections that follow.

1. USE OPEN-ENDED RATHER THAN CLOSE-ENDED QUESTIONS.

An open-ended question "opens up" the discussion to wider exploration. A close-ended question "closes" the discussion to deciding between agreement or disagreement. The following are contrasting examples.

- "What are the advantages and disadvantages of labor unions?" versus "Are you for or against labor unions?"
- "When are statistics useful and when can they be misleading?" versus "Do statistics lie?"
- "What did you like about *To Kill a Mockingbird*?" versus "Did you like *To Kill a Mockingbird*?"

The only time a close-ended question might be a better choice is when you want to poll students or spark a debate.

2. MAKE THE WORDING OF A QUESTION CLEAR.

Your words may be clear to you but not to your students for two reasons: (1) they are open to different interpretations and (2) your language might not be your students' language. The following are some examples in which the wording may need to be improved.

- A teacher asks: "What should the role of the media be?" Unfortunately, the word *media* is quite broad. Some students will think the teacher is referring to newspapers while others will assume the term means radio, TV, or reporting on the Internet.
- A teacher asks: "How should we deal with the energy crisis?" The teacher's focus might be on the question "How should we conserve energy?" but the students might focus instead on the question "How can we develop alternative sources of energy?"
- A teacher asks: "What do you think accounts for fluctuations in the international monetary system?" Several students can't relate to the phrase "fluctuations in the international monetary system" but would know immediately what was meant if the teacher were to ask "Why do you think the U.S. dollar is worth more in some years when you travel to other countries but is worth less in other years?"

3. LIMIT THE NUMBER OF QUESTIONS.

It's usually better to ask just one or two questions at a time. Students lose focus when you give them too much to ponder. If you have a follow-up question, it's better to ask it later rather than at the same time as the initial question. Furthermore, don't give more than one version of the same question, hoping that one of your versions clicks. Take the time beforehand to compose the question as effectively as possible.

4. ESTABLISH YOUR GOALS AND OBJECTIVES.

Your discussions will be more focused if you think through what you want the discussion to accomplish. For example, do you want students to debate or to reflect? to make a decision or to explore options? to increase their doubt or to shore up their determination? to broaden their thinking or to concretize it? Although you can't "legislate" the outcomes of any discussion, how you guide it may influence what happens to your students at the end. The following are two examples.

- The topic is human cloning, but what is the goal? One teacher decides that he wants the discussion to enhance his students' understanding of the variety of viewpoints on the topic. Accordingly, the discussion is not focused on whether it's a good idea or bad idea but rather on appreciating the various perspectives that ordinary people, religious leaders, and scientists have on human cloning.

- The topic is homelessness, but what is the goal? One teacher decides that she wants her students to discuss if people are homeless by choice or by fortune. She begins the discussion by playing audiotape interviews of three homeless individuals. She then asks her students to share their reactions to the interview, focusing on two questions: Why are these individuals currently homeless? Why are these individuals choosing not to live in shelters?

PLANNING SHEET

State Effective Questions for Discussion

Use the following sheet to implement this strategy.

Technique (check one or more):

_____ Use open-ended rather than close-ended questions.

_____ Make the wording of a question clear.

_____ Limit the number of questions.

_____ Establish your goals and objectives.

My Plan:

_____

_____

_____

_____

_____

_____

_____

_____

_____

_____

_____

_____

_____

_____

_____

_____

_____

STRATEGY #11:
Improve the Quality of Discussion through Student Preparation

The expression "garbage in, garbage out" applies here. Students, especially the opinionated ones, too often talk "garbage" in the sense that they have little to back up what they are saying. However, if teachers don't push students to get the facts and to think more critically before they spout their opinions they contribute to the "garbage in." Of course, there are many other students who hold back in discussions when they might be willing to participate if they first have a chance to obtain information and think before they talk. Let's explore ways to get more students to participate and improve the quality of discussion as well.

1. LET STUDENTS "PRE-DISCUSS."

Place students in pairs or trios and present your discussion topic and question(s). Ask them to talk with each other briefly before you open up the discussion to the entire class.

You might say, for example:

Some politicians believe that we should have a flat rather than a progressive income tax. They believe that it would be more effective if everyone was taxed at the same rate rather than having different tax brackets, depending on how rich or poor one is. Get together with your partner and talk about your views on the matter for a few minutes. Maybe you both have a lot to say, so give each other a chance to speak. Maybe one of you knows more about this topic and can share that knowledge with your partner. Maybe you both are unsure what to say. Try to figure out what the consequences of each system might be. Do your best. We'll get together as a whole class in three minutes.

The opportunity to "rehearse" what they might say in the full group will give more students than usual the courage to participate. The "pre-discussion" also helps them to warm up to the topic and get them thinking in advance of going public.

2. "SNOWBALL" THE PARTICIPATION.

To ease your students gradually into full group discussion, you can have pre-discussion in pairs and then combine pairs into quartets (and even "snowball" into groups of eight, if time allows). Introduce any discussion question appropriate to your class. Explain the "snowball discussion" design, if you wish, at the start of the process, or make it a surprise.

The following outlines a plan for a snowball discussion that lasts for 50 minutes.

1. Pair up students and ask them to discuss a question for *two minutes*.

2. Ask pairs to form quartets. (If there is an odd pair, have them join one of the quartets.) Give them *three minutes* to exchange ideas. Ask each quartet to appoint a spokesperson for the next round.

3. Combine quartets into octets. (If there is an odd quartet, have them join one of the octets.) Give them *15 minutes* to hear from each quartet spokesperson and react to the ideas given. Select a spokesperson to report on the octet discussion.

4. Allow 30 minutes for full class discussion and closure.

3. PROVIDE BACKGROUND INFORMATION OR ARGUMENTS.

You can assist students in preparing for a high-quality discussion by giving them data that might shed more light than heat in the discussion to follow. Options include:

- *A fact sheet:* Data on the number of jobs that have been outsourced in certain industries to workers outside the United States
- *Brief opinions:* Four quotations from well-known personalities on standards of decency in radio and television
- *Debate points:* A brief list of pro and con arguments on a controversial topic such as abortion
- *Case example(s):* Two examples of parliamentary government

When you use this approach, give your students the data before class or right before the discussion. Give them time to read, to discuss the information with peers, and to ask questions toward clarifying the content.

4. ASK STUDENTS TO DO THEIR OWN RESEARCH.

The best way to enhance the quantity and quality of discussion participation is to invite or require students to collect information that enables them to be an informed participant. The following are examples.

- Students are asked to obtain information from government web sites to participate in a discussion on disease control policies.
- Students are required to poll their friends and family about the question "What would you save first if your home were on fire?"
- Students are encouraged to read the reporting of two different newspapers regarding the same event or issue.
- Students are invited to interview their family doctor about his or her concerns about medical malpractice insurance.

PLANNING SHEET

Improve the Quality of Discussion through Student Participation

Use the following sheet to implement this strategy.

Technique (check one or more):

_____ Let students "pre-discuss."

_____ "Snowball" the participation.

_____ Provide background information or arguments.

_____ Ask students to do their own research.

My Plan:

_____

_____

_____

_____

_____

_____

_____

_____

_____

_____

_____

_____

_____

_____

_____

_____

STRATEGY #12:
Match the Discussion Format to the Situation

Generally speaking, a wide-open discussion is a poor format for obtaining high participation and focused conversation. As discussed previously, open discussion often yields few participants. You get to hear from four or five students who do most of the talking in class. If you are concerned that new people will not participate, remember to say, "How many of you want to give your opinion?" rather than "Who wants to start us off?"

If you are lucky enough to have a very participative group, that's great, unless you are worried that the discussion might drag on by the time you allow everyone to speak. To preserve time, say beforehand, "I'd like to ask four or five students to share." In place of or in addition to open discussion, there are many other options. The following sections explore some of them.

1. USE RESPONSE CARDS.

Pass out index cards and request anonymous answers to your question. Use response cards to save time, to provide anonymity for personally threatening self-disclosures, or to make it easier for shy people to contribute. The need to state yourself concisely on a card is another advantage of this method. Say, "For this discussion, I would like you to write down your thoughts first before we talk together any further." Have the index cards passed around the group or have them returned to you to be read at a later point. Be careful to make your question clear and to encourage brief, legible responses.

2. FORM SUBGROUPS OF THREE OR MORE.

Use subgroup discussions when you have sufficient time to discuss issues in depth. This is one of the key methods for obtaining everyone's participation. You can assign students to subgroups randomly (e.g., by counting off) or purposefully (e.g., by forming an all-female group). Pose a question for discussion or give the subgroup a task or assignment to complete. It is often helpful to designate group roles such as facilitator, timekeeper, recorder, or presenter, and to obtain volunteers or assign members to fill them. Make sure that students are in face-to-face contact with each other. Try to separate subgroups so that they do not disturb each other.

3. HAVE DISCUSSION IN PAIRS.

Couple students for both a brief exchange (even one minute) or a longer dialogue. Use pairs when you want to involve everybody. Create student partners either by physical proximity or by a wish to put certain individuals together. You can ask pairs to do many things, such as reading and discussing a short written document together, developing or responding to a question, or comparing their ideas to those of some activity they performed previously on an independent basis. Give instructions such as: "Read this handout together and discuss it. Come up with examples or applications of what you are reading." "Create a question you both have about this topic." "Discuss together your response to the following question." "Compare your results on this survey. How are your views alike or different?"

4. GO AROUND THE CLASS AND OBTAIN SHORT RESPONSES.

Use this method when you want to obtain something quickly from each student. Sentence stems (e.g., "One thing that makes a good scientist is _____") are useful in conducting go-arounds. Invite students to "pass" when they wish. Avoid repetition by asking each student for a new contribution to the process. If the group is large, create a smaller go-around group by obtaining short responses from one side of the room, from people who are wearing glasses, or from some other subsection of the class.

5. HAVE STUDENTS CALL ON ONE ANOTHER.

Ask students to raise a hand when they want to share their views, and ask the present speaker in the group (not the teacher) to call on the next speaker. Say, "For this discussion, I would like you to call on each other rather than having me select who is to speak next. When you have finished speaking, look around to see whose hands are raised and call on someone." (Do not allow students to call on people who have not indicated a desire to participate.) Use calling on the next speaker when you are sure there is a lot of interest in the discussion or activity and you wish to promote student-to-student interaction. When you wish to resume as moderator, inform the group that you are changing back to the regular format.

6. CREATE DISCUSSION PANELS.

Invite a small number of students to present their views in front of the entire class. Use panels when time permits to have a focused, serious response to your discussion questions. Rotate panelists to increase participation. An informal panel can be created by asking for the views of a designated number of students who remain in their seats. Serve as panel moderator or invite a student to perform this role.

A variation of a panel discussion is a "fishbowl" discussion. A fishbowl is a type of rotating panel. Ask a portion of the class to form a discussion circle and have the remaining students form a listening circle around them. Use a fishbowl to help bring focus to large-group discussions. Although it is time consuming, this is the best method for combining the virtues of large- and small-group discussion. Bring new groups into the inner circle to continue the discussion. You can do this by obtaining new volunteers or assigning students to be discussants.

Bear in mind that you can combine some of these six discussion formats. For example, you might pose a question, form partners to discuss it, and then obtain whole-group reaction through methods such as open discussion, calling on the next speaker, and panels. By inserting the partner exchange first, you will have more people ready to participate in the whole-group setting. Alternatively, begin with response cards, followed by a go-around or subgroups.

7. STAGE A DEBATE.

You can also hold an "active debate" that involves every participant in the class, not just the debaters. Steps for doing so follow.

1. Develop a statement that takes a position with regard to a controversial issue relating to your subject matter (e.g., "The pharmaceutical industry has been irresponsible about reporting negative results").

2. Divide the class into two debating teams. Arbitrarily assign the "pro" position to one group and the "con" position to the other.

3. Create two to four subgroupings within each debating team. In a class of 24 students, for example, you might create three "pro" subgroups and three "con" subgroups, each containing four members. Ask each subgroup to develop arguments for its assigned position. At the end of their discussion, have each subgroup select a spokesperson.

4. Set up two to four chairs (depending on the number of subgroups created for each side) for the spokespersons on the "pro" side and, facing them, the same number of chairs for the spokespersons on the "con" side. Place the remaining students behind their debate team. Begin the "debate" by having the spokespersons present their views. Refer to this process as "opening arguments."

5. After everyone has heard the opening arguments, stop the debate and reconvene the original subgroups. Ask the subgroups to strategize how to counter the opening arguments of the opposing side. Again, have each subgroup select a spokesperson, preferably a new person.

6. Resume the "debate." Have the spokespersons, seated across from each other, give "counterarguments." As the debate continues (be sure to alternate between both sides), encourage other students to pass notes to their debaters with suggested arguments or rebuttals. Also, urge them to cheer or applaud the arguments of their debate team representatives.

7. When you think it appropriate, end the debate. Instead of declaring a winner, reconvene the entire class in a single circle. Be sure to "integrate" the class by having students sit next to those who were on opposite sides. Hold a classwide discussion on what the students learned about the issue from the debate experience. Also, ask students to identify what they thought were the best arguments raised on both sides.

You can also use a debate format that is less formal and moves more quickly. This works as follows.

1. Select an issue that has two or more sides.

2. Divide the class according to the number of positions you have stated and ask each group to come up with arguments that support their position. Encourage students to work with seat partners or small cluster groups.

3. Seat groups opposite each other.

4. Explain that any participant can begin the debate. After that participant has had an opportunity to present one argument in favor of his or her assigned position, allow a different argument or counterargument from another group. Continue the discussion, moving quickly back and forth between the groups.

5. Conclude the activity by comparing the issues as you see them. Allow for follow-up reaction and discussion.

PLANNING SHEET

Match the Discussion Format to the Situation
Use the following sheet to implement this strategy.

Technique (check one or more):

_____ Use response cards.

_____ Form subgroups of three or more.

_____ Have discussion in pairs.

_____ Go around the class and obtain short responses.

_____ Have students call on one another.

_____ Create discussion panels.

_____ Stage a debate.

My Plan:

_____

_____

_____

_____

_____

_____

_____

_____

_____

_____

_____

_____

_____

STRATEGY #13:
Facilitate the Flow of Conversation
....

Some of the discussion options just presented allow you to sit back and let the students take charge. Other options require your leadership. In such cases, your role is to facilitate the flow of comments from students. Although it is not necessary to make an interjection after each person speaks, periodically assisting students with their contributions can be helpful. The following is a ten-point facilitation menu to select from as you lead group discussions.

1. PARAPHRASE.

You can feed back what someone has said so that the student knows that she or he has been understood and the other students can hear a concise summary of what has just been said.

> "So what you're saying is that we have to be very careful about the words we use because a particular person might be offended by them."

2. CHECK.

Check your understanding against the words of a student, or ask a student to clarify what she or he is saying.

> "Are you saying that this political correctness has gone too far? I'm not sure that I understand exactly what you meant."

3. COMPLIMENT.

Do this in regard to an interesting or insightful comment.

> "That's a good point. I'm glad you brought it to our attention."

4. ELABORATE.

Elaborate on a student's contribution to the discussion with examples or suggest a new way of viewing the problem.

> "Your comments provide an interesting point from the teenage perspective. We could also consider how a senior citizen would view the same situation."

5. ENERGIZE.

You can energize discussion by quickening the pace, using humor, or if necessary, prodding the class for more contributions.

"Oh my, we have lots of quiet people in this class! Here's a challenge for you. For the next two minutes, let's see how many terms you can think of that are no longer socially acceptable."

6. DISAGREE.

Do this (gently) with a student's comments to stimulate further discussion.

"I can see where you're coming from, but I'm not sure that what you are describing is always the case. Has anyone else had an experience that's different from Jennifer's?"

7. MEDIATE.

Mediate differences of opinion between students and relieve any tensions that may be brewing.

"Darryl and Shaun . . . I think you are not really disagreeing with each other but are just bringing out two different sides of this issue."

8. PULL TOGETHER.

Pull together ideas, showing their relationship to each other.

"As you can see from the comments of Samantha and Richard, the words we use can offend people. Both of them have given us an example of how they feel excluded by gender-based words."

9. CHANGE.

Change the group process by altering the method of participation or prompting the group to evaluate ideas that have been raised during the previous discussion.

"Let's break into smaller groups and see if you can come up with some suggestions for establishing gender-sensitive word usage."

10. SUMMARIZE.

Summarize (and record, if desired) the major views of the class.

"I have noted three major reasons that have come from this discussion as to when words are harmful: (1) they exclude some people, (2) they insult some people, and (3) they are determined only by the majority culture."

Any of these facilitating behaviors can be used alone or in conjunction with the others to help stimulate discussions within your class. As students become more and more relaxed about contributing their ideas and opinions, you can shift from being a leader to being an occasional facilitator, and perhaps even another person with an opinion. As your role in the conversation diminishes, the students make the discussion their own.

PLANNING SHEET

Facilitate the Flow of Conversation
Use the following sheet to implement this strategy.

Technique (check one or more):

_____ Paraphrase.

_____ Check.

_____ Compliment.

_____ Elaborate.

_____ Energize.

_____ Disagree.

_____ Mediate.

_____ Pull together.

_____ Change.

_____ Summarize.

My Plan:

_____

_____

_____

_____

_____

_____

_____

_____

_____

_____

_____

_____

_____

....

Urge Students to Ask Questions

The act of learning begins with a question. The brain starts the work of learning because it has a question about information it is obtaining from the senses (hearing, sight, touch, and taste) that feed it. If the brain could talk, it would say things such as: *Where does this information fit? Does it confirm what I already know? Does it challenge what I already know?* If the brain isn't curious about incoming information, it takes the path of least resistance; that is, it attends to something else.

Urging students to inquire means getting them to ask questions. When students are asking questions, they are in a seeking mode rather than a passive mode. Their brains are activated to obtain answers rather than merely "logging in." For example, if students are asked to read some information or view presentation slides and they come to it with few or no questions, their brains treat the information superficially. If they are trying to find out something, their brains treat the information carefully.

Getting students to ask questions is easier said than done. Many students are so used to being told or shown things that they become consumers rather than seekers of knowledge. As a result, they may have few questions except "Will this be on the test?" Furthermore, many teachers are so accustomed to *asking* students questions (e.g., "What's an example of that? How did you arrive at that answer?") that they forget to inquire of students if they have any questions of their own. As a result, students often receive little practice asking questions.

This is ironic, because when they were young children they asked questions all the time. "Why, Mommy, why?" was, perhaps, their first formal question. Even before they could verbalize a question, they were seeking information from everything they did. For example, putting every object into his or her mouth is the way an infant finds out how something tastes, if it is hard or soft, or if it will produce milk. Touching everything in sight is a way in which a toddler explores what's in the world.

Despite their early curiosity, you may be highly pessimistic that your students will ask questions at this point in their lives. For example, if you have invited your entire class to ask you questions about the material you have been teaching, it is likely that you have been met with repeated silence or only obtained questions from a few students. Moreover, any questions you have gotten may have been poorly formed. If you have approached students individually with an openness to answering their questions, you may have also been met with resistance. Imagine, for instance, that a student tells you he can't do a math problem you have assigned. If you ask him "What don't you understand about it?" or "Where are you having difficulty?" the student might just shrug his shoulders, as if responding "Darned if I know."

Because these realities are so pervasive, I would like to suggest four strategies that will help you overcome this resistance and encourage your students to become more eager inquirers. These strategies follow.

STRATEGY #14:
Help Students Get Started

Because students have so little practice in asking questions, they may need a lot of help in getting started. The following are some suggestions.

1. GIVE STUDENTS A LIST OF QUESTIONS AS A REFERENCE.

Providing questions is a great way of easing students into question asking. Instead of asking them for potential questions, give your students a list of questions (two to eight questions) about the topic or material you want them to inquire about. Be sure your questions are not too sophisticated. They should sound like questions curious students (not teachers!) would state. Ask students to vote for questions they'd like you to answer. After giving them such a list a few times, your students should gain some insights into how to raise questions. At that point, switch to asking them to generate their own questions.

2. ASK STUDENTS TO DEVELOP A QUESTION WITH A PARTNER.

It's much easier to generate questions from students if they work with a partner first. There are two ways to do this. One way is to give each student some time to think of a question (and write it down) and share the question with a partner. With two possible questions, the pair could choose one of the two to submit, or combine them into one question. (If one student can't think of a question, the partner's question can be submitted.) The second way is to have the student pairs convene right from the beginning and compose a question together.

3. TEACH STUDENTS HOW TO ASK GOOD QUESTIONS.

You can help students generate good questions if they understand and practice how to create some. You might begin by teaching students how to signal to themselves that something needs clarification. To build this awareness, try two ideas. One is to ask students to read something with a highlighter pen in hand. Tell them *not* to highlight text they already understand. Instead, ask them to highlight text that raises questions for them. Then, ask them to go over what they've highlighted and write down phrases they would like clarified—or if possible an actual question about the highlighted material. The other idea is to ask students to keep a card or piece of paper accessible while they are listening to a lecture or class discussion and to write down any questions that come to mind.

Once students build conscious awareness of questions, you can then spend some time teaching them to distinguish between low-quality and high-quality questions. For example, yes/no questions are not as helpful as open-ended questions, specific questions are usually better than broad questions, and clear questions are better than confusing questions. One technique is to give them a comparative list of examples, as in the following.

Poor Question	*Better Question*
Is Wal-Mart a good company? (a yes/no question)	What are the advantages and disadvantages of working at Wal-Mart?
What do you think of chocolate? (an unclear and broad question)	Does chocolate have any health benefits?

You might follow this with a list of poor questions and ask students to improve them on their own.

4. MODEL GOOD QUESTIONS.

You serve as a positive model when you ask your students probing questions. One interesting way to do this is to use a technique I call Role-Reversal Questions. Compose questions you would raise about some learning material *if you were a student*. Create questions that have the following properties.

- Seek to clarify difficult or complex material (e.g., "Would you explain again the way to _____?")
- Compare the material to other information (e.g., "How is this different from _____?")
- Challenge your own points of view (e.g., "Why is it necessary to do this? Wouldn't it lead to a lot of confusion?")
- Request examples of the ideas being discussed (e.g., "Could you give me an example of _____?")
- Test the applicability of the material (e.g., "How could I use this idea in real life?")

At the beginning of a question period, announce to the students that you are going to "be" them, and they collectively are going to "be" you. Proceed to ask your questions.

Be argumentative, humorous, and whatever else it takes to get them to jump into the fray and bombard you with answers. Reversing roles a few times will keep your students on their toes and prompt them to ask questions on their own.

Another technique is called Planted Questions. This technique enables you to present information in response to questions that have been "planted" with selected students. Although you are, in effect, giving a well-prepared lesson, it appears to other students that you are merely conducting a question-and-answer session.

Choose questions that will guide your lesson. Write three to six questions and sequence them logically. List each on an index card, and write down the cue you will use to signal you want that question asked. Cues you might use include the following.

- Scratching your nose
- Taking off your eyeglasses
- Snapping your fingers
- Yawning

Prior to the lesson, select the students who will ask the questions. Give each an index card, and explain their cue. Make sure they do not reveal to anyone else that they are "plants." Open the question-and-answer session by announcing the topic and giving your first clue. Call on the first "plant," answer the question, and then continue with the rest of the cues and questions. Next, open the floor to new questions; that is, questions not previously "planted." It is likely that several hands will go up.

PLANNING SHEET

Help Students Get Started

Use the following sheet to implement this strategy.

Technique (check one or more):

_____ Give students a list of questions as a reference.

_____ Ask students to develop a question with a partner.

_____ Teach students how to ask good questions.

_____ Model good questions.

My Plan:

_____

_____

_____

_____

_____

_____

_____

_____

_____

_____

_____

_____

_____

_____

STRATEGY #15:
Create the Need for Questions

....

Many teachers stifle question-asking by "covering everything." What this means is that loading students with information overloads their brains and leaves them with little energy to discover good questions. As stated previously, when you *cover* too much students have little need to *uncover* anything for themselves. The following are some ideas for creating the need for questions by covering less.

1. ASK STUDENTS TO INTERPRET AMBIGUOUS INFORMATION.

Distribute to students a handout that provides broad information but lacks details or explanatory backup. An interesting chart or diagram that illustrates information is also a good choice. A text that's open to interpretation is another option. The goal is to evoke curiosity.

Ask students to study the handout with a partner. Request that each pair make as much sense of the material as possible and then identify what they do not understand *by marking up the document with questions next to information they do not understand*. Encourage students to insert as many question marks as they wish. If time permits, form pairs into quartets and allow time for each pair to help the other.

A physics teacher, for example, might distribute a diagram illustrating how potential energy converts to kinetic energy as represented by a circus diver leaping from a 50-foot pole. Students work with a partner to review the illustration and arrive at questions (e.g., When, exactly, does the potential energy become kinetic energy? What is the basic difference between kinetic and potential energy?).

Reconvene the class and field questions that students have. In essence, you are teaching through your answers to student questions rather than through a preset lesson. Alternatively, listen to the questions all together and then teach a preset lesson, making special efforts to respond to the questions students pose. If you feel that students will be lost trying to study the material entirely on their own, provide some information that orients them or gives them the basic knowledge they need to be able to inquire on their own. Just be careful not to cover too much ground. Then, proceed with obtaining their questions.

2. GIVE STUDENTS A JOB TO DO THAT FORCES THEM TO ASK QUESTIONS.

In this technique, students are given realistic on-the-job assignments with little prior instruction. Choose the role you want students to perform. The following are some examples.

I am the
mayor

visitor to _____ [foreign country]

editor

historian

scientist

job applicant

business owner

researcher

journalist

Prepare written instructions explaining one or several tasks that might be assigned to that role. For example, a mayor might be asked to bring a bill to the city council. Pair up students and present the assignments to each pair. Give them a specified period of time to figure out what information they need and what questions they have in order to complete the job. Then, provide them with the reference material they need to support them as they attempt to deal with the assignments.

3. HAVE STUDENTS BRAINSTORM QUESTIONS.

Another technique that encourages question asking is "brainstorming." Typically, brainstorming activities require students to generate several ideas or solutions. It's also possible to have them brainstorm questions. Give students a topic. Some examples are:

- Heart disease
- The Bill of Rights
- AIDS
- Nuclear proliferation
- Tort reform
- Jane Austen
- The Crusades

Place students in small groups and ask them to generate as many questions as they can about that topic. You might have them imagine they are preparing to interview an expert on the topic and must have a list of questions to use. If you wish, you can create a contest in which the group that develops the most questions wins. After groups present their questions, have students choose which questions they feel are the best ones and why.

4. INVITE STUDENTS TO CREATE QUESTIONS FOR CLASS DISCUSSION.

Give students the responsibility of leading class discussion. Give them a topic for discussion, but leave it up to them to identify discussion questions. The following is an interesting example from a class on the Bible.

Students are given the Biblical verse "Honor Your Father and Mother" and are asked to develop up to five questions for class discussion. Working in small groups, they identify some potential questions and then vote on the best ones. The final list of questions might be:

- *What does "honor" mean when you are 10 years old? 20? 40? 60?*
- *Why should you "honor" your parents? Does the Bible give a reason?*
- *Who else besides parents should children honor?*
- *How do you honor a parent who didn't raise you?*
- *What if the parent has been irresponsible? abusive?*

PLANNING SHEET

Create the Need for Questions

Use the following sheet to implement this strategy.

Technique (check one or more)

_____ Ask students to interpret ambiguous information.

_____ Give students a job to do that forces them to ask questions.

_____ Have students brainstorm questions.

_____ Invite students to create questions for class discussion.

My Plan:

_____

_____

_____

_____

_____

_____

_____

_____

_____

_____

_____

_____

_____

_____

STRATEGY #16:
Let Students Know You Expect Questions

Go beyond merely encouraging your students to ask questions. Push them to ask questions. The following sections discuss ways to demonstrate that you expect questions from them.

1. BEGIN EACH CLASS WITH A QUESTION-AND-ANSWER SESSION.

Inform your students that you will set aside a few minutes at the start of your next class to answer questions they have about (select one or more categories):

- Material covered in the last class session
- Homework assignments
- Reading in preparation for today's class

Urge students to come to class with questions. Explain to them that asking questions is important to their educational development.

The first class session during which you start with a question-and-answer activity will probably not produce widespread participation. Perhaps only a few students will have questions. Don't be dismayed. Persist. After the second or third time, your students will begin to believe that you really mean it when you say you expect questions. They will begin the practice of thinking before coming to class. As a result, the number of actual questions you receive will increase over time. Continue this activity for as long as you wish.

2. END EACH CLASS WITH A QUESTION-AND-ANSWER SESSION.

Use the same process described previously, but invite student questions at the end of class. Again, be persistent. Over time, students will start thinking about questions during class. (And wouldn't that be wonderful?)

3. REQUIRE STUDENTS TO SUBMIT QUESTIONS TO YOU.

Consider giving students an assignment in which they must develop questions about the material you are teaching. Give them clear instructions. For example, you might say: "At the beginning of our next class, I want you to give me two or three questions you have about Act II, Scene 3, of *Macbeth*. The questions can be about such matters as the meaning of certain lines, the character's motives, or Shakespeare's literary devices. Take your time composing the questions, as I am going to grade you on their quality. The better your questions the better your grade." Provide examples of good and poor questions about a previous scene from the play.

PLANNING SHEET

Let Students Know You Expect Questions

Use the following sheet to implement this strategy.

Technique (check one or more):

_____ Begin each class with a question-and-answer session.

_____ End each class with a question-and-answer session.

_____ Require students to submit questions to you.

My Plan:

_____

_____

_____

_____

_____

_____

_____

_____

_____

_____

_____

_____

_____

_____

_____

_____

_____

Let Your Students Learn from Each Other

You might think it risky to put students in small groups for extended periods of time. The risk may be worth it. Your students can learn as much from each other as they can learn from you. After all, they "speak each other's language." They can also give each other more personal attention than you can give to each of them. Under the right conditions, learning that is collaborative is more active than learning that is teacher led.

In educational jargon, students learning from each other is referred to by such terms as *cooperative/collaborative learning, group learning, peer tutoring,* and *peer teaching.* I will use the term *team learning* because it suggests that a team effort is needed for learning results to occur. Students need to think "we" rather than "me."

Team learning has many benefits. Students develop a bond with their learning teammates that may motivate the team to sustain collaborative learning activity through complex, challenging assignments. Further, students in learning teams are willing to accept greater responsibility for their own development precisely because they have a sense of ownership and social support. Think how often you say to yourself the phrase "my class." Teachers naturally have a sense that they "own" their classroom when they say such things as "I hope my class goes well today," or "in my class, students are well behaved." When team learning is happening, students get the feeling that it's *their* class.

Unfortunately, team learning also has its drawbacks. Chief among these is the fact that teachers have less instructional control than when they themselves are front and center. Have any of the following things ever happened to you when you have put students in learning groups for short or long periods of time?

- *Confusion:* Students don't know what to do because they didn't understand or follow the directions.

- *Tangents:* Students don't stick to the topic and get off task.

- *Unequal participation:* Some students dominate; some remain quiet.

- *One-way communication:* Students don't listen to or respond to each other.

- *No division of labor:* Some students don't pull their own weight. They let the team down, and are not dependable.

- *Superficiality:* The team is done before you know it, breezing through the assignment in the fastest way possible and staying on the surface rather than digging below it.

Chances are you have experienced nearly all of these problems, in both short- and long-term groups. When they happen, students and teachers alike get turned off to team learning. What can be done?

STRATEGY #17:
Choose How You Compose Learning Teams

How you compose learning teams is often critical to team-learning success. The following explore several considerations.

1. KEEP THE LEARNING UNIT SMALL.

The first consideration in promoting team learning is the size of the teams. In my experience, productive teams can range from two to six members. Small teams work faster and can manage and coordinate their work with greater ease. Teams that are larger than six members have the advantage of greater knowledge, skill, and perspectives. They can cope with larger projects and can cover for missing or slack members. But large teams often get bogged down in group process issues that prevent them from moving forward. They are difficult to organize, and it can be especially difficult to pull together the work of a large team. If you still wish to use teams larger than six members, be aware that such teams need more structure, more formal meetings, and clearer roles for each member than small teams.

It's a good idea to vary the size of the teams at different times. Sometimes, use pairs. Other times, use trios, quartets, quintets, or sextets. Remember that you can "snowball" pairs into quartets or trios into groups of six. Your students will learn more about teamwork if they work in groups of different sizes, and they are less likely to complain about who is in their group.

2. GAIN THE ADVANTAGES OF RANDOM ASSIGNMENT.

There are two benefits to forming teams by leaving it up to chance. One benefit is that students can't gravitate to their friends or only to those with whom they are comfortable. (Although self-selected grouping can work out at times, the greater risk is that friends will socialize more than you prefer.) The other benefit is that students can't exclude one another. Through random assignment, students usually wind up with some classmates whom they don't know well or who may be more or less knowledgeable than they. It's a very powerful message to say to your students that, in effect, they are expected to work with anyone and everyone in the class.

The simplest way to assign students randomly is by "counting off." Count the number of students as soon as you believe you have full attendance. Then determine how large your subgroups will be by finding a number that easily divides into your total number of students. Be careful. For example, if you have 24 students and you want groups with four members, ask students to count off by sixes (1, 2, 3, 4, 5, 6; 1, 2, 3, 4, 5, 6; etc.). If you count off by fours, you'll wind up with four groups of six students. If the total number of students is not an even number or a number that can be divided evenly, be aware that typically one or more groups will have one fewer member than the others. For example, in a class of 25 students you have the possibility of five groups of five students, but if you want quartets you will have five groups of four students and one group of five students.

There are several other methods of random assignment, such as grouping students with similar birthdays or first initials, or randomly giving students cards, stickers, or dots of varying color or having them pick these items out of a hat.

3. COMPOSE DIVERSE GROUPS.

When you assign students randomly, there is a likelihood but no guarantee you'll obtain diverse groups (by gender, race, IQ, knowledge, motivation, and so forth). You are more likely to obtain the diversity you may be seeking by deliberately composing the teams yourself. Diverse teams take longer to get started, but often succeed in the long run because of the richness of their resources. There are other reasons to form diverse teams, such as the following.

- You want to be sure that there is at least one skilled or "responsible" student in each team.
- You want different points of view.
- You want to make sure that every student has someone on whom he or she can rely for support. (For example, you can compose teams so that every member has the strong possibility of having one "friend.")

You need to know your class well if you are to use diverse groups effectively. Therefore, it's a strategy that works best after several class sessions. My favorite way of forming diverse groups is as follows. Arrange the seating in a classroom before the students arrive into the group configurations you desire (e.g., tables for six students) and place name tents or name cards on the seats or desktops at each team location. As students enter the classroom, have them find their seats. Some students may grumble when they discover that there are assigned seats (especially if they don't like the group they are placed in), but they usually survive if you are unwavering about your decision. If students have preexisting assigned seats, of course, you will have to ask them to take other seats for the time allocated to team learning.

If you can't arrange assigned seating before class, you will need to ask your students to change seats once they arrive. A friendly way to pull this off is to tell your students you have created teams for today's class (the teams can continue for more than one class session) and that these teams are designated by a letter (e.g., Team A) or by a name (e.g., a U.S. President, an animal, or a car). Then, announce the names of the members of each team. When composing teams for diversity, consider the following possibilities.

- Put together students who don't know each other.
- Choose students who balance each other in terms of learning style and motivation.
- Mix students by gender, race, age, or other significant category.

4. CREATE HOMOGENEOUS GROUPS.

On occasion, it may be best to form teams by assigning members who share an important attribute. Homogeneous teams tend to organize themselves quickly and obtain immediate results. Such a grouping may also be useful when you have some students who need extra help. By putting them together in one group, you are then able to give those students extra assistance and support. Some types of homogeneous groupings you might use are:

- Students with common interests
- Students who share a common background, work experience, and so forth
- Students of similar skills or learning style

You can also employ any of the suggestions for assigning students to groups that were mentioned previously with regard to diverse grouping (e.g., place cards).

5. ALLOW STUDENTS TO CHOOSE THEIR OWN GROUPS.

For the many reasons previously alluded to, it is risky to let students choose their own groups when a sustained team effort is required. However, there are some circumstances when it may be the wise thing to do. For example, you may already have evidence that self-selected groups have been successful when you have had brief periods of group activity in your class. Now you want to launch more serious team learning activities and believe that you can trust students to group themselves. You may also be willing to go along with students' wishes to choose their own groups if the friendship groups of the class are somewhat firmly established and you are willing to let things be and see how the situation works out. If you allow students to choose their own groups, be careful about the following.

- Keep the teams to a similar size.
- Preserve your option to modify the groups if some don't work out or if some students get excluded.
- Monitor excessive socializing.

PLANNING SHEET

Choose How You Compose Learning Teams
Use the following sheet to implement this strategy.

Technique (check one or more):

_____ Keep the learning unit small.

_____ Gain the advantages of random assignment.

_____ Compose diverse groups.

_____ Create homogeneous groups.

_____ Allow students to choose their own groups.

My Plan:

_____

_____

_____

_____

_____

_____

_____

_____

_____

_____

_____

_____

_____

_____

_____

_____

_____

_____

STRATEGY #18:
Build Learning Teams before Giving Students Work

Once learning teams have been assigned, it's probably a good idea to have them experience some initial team building. From everything we know about group development, teams can't *perform* until they have a chance to *form*. This axiom applies big-time to classroom groups. Students need the opportunity to get comfortable with each other before they take on the responsibility of doing their own learning. They also need to bond socially and get accustomed to working as a group without the direct guidance of the teacher.

How much time you allocate to the team-building process depends on your personal circumstances. For some teachers, it may be no more than 20 minutes. For others, it may be several hours. In my view, however much time you take will be recovered many times over once you see the difference some initial team building makes. Let's explore some ways of spending this time wisely.

1. UTILIZE TEAM-BUILDING ACTIVITIES.

There are numerous structured activities that help to form teams. These activities help teams get to know each other rapidly and build a degree of team cohesion early on. The following are three examples.

- *Predictions:* In each group, give students three to five questions a person might ask about himself or herself, such as: "What type of _____ (music, art, sports, games, people) do I like?" "What is my favorite _____ (ice cream, novel, TV program, leisure activity)?" "What is my opinion about _____ (hip-hop, God, our President, working in teams)?" Ask each student to take a turn asking these questions to other members of their learning team. After team members guess the answer(s) to each question, have the student inform the others what is true for him or her.

- *Group résumé:* Ask each team to compose a group résumé. Give the groups newsprint and markers to display their résumés. The résumés should include any data that sells the group as a whole. Included can be information about members' skills, accomplishments, work experience, education, and hobbies. Invite each group to present its résumé to the rest of the class.

- *Ball toss:* Give each team a ball and have them form a circle. Ask team members to toss the ball to each other so that each person has the ball only once and that the person who starts the sequence cannot toss the ball to a person to his or her immediate right or left. (This last direction requires a group of at least four students.) For example, in a group of five, person 1 can toss to person 3, who tosses to person 5, who tosses to person 2, who tosses to person 4. Once the sequence has been completed, challenge the group to repeat it faster and faster. If you wish, tell them that the ball does not have to be tossed, but it must be touched by only one person at a time and must be exchanged in the same order of people. The challenge can lead to many creative ideas, and groups can increase the speed of the process to the point of taking only one second!

2. GIVE STUDENTS A BRIEF TASTE OF TEAM LEARNING.

It's important for students to experience learning from each other without the direction of a teacher not only to develop an image of what is expected later on but to have some immediate success. The following are some ways of accomplishing this.

- Give teams one simple but provocative question to answer (e.g., "Who is the hero of this story?").
- Give teams one sentence to discuss or interpret (e.g., "Every vote counts.").
- Give teams one short task to accomplish together (e.g., the translation of one paragraph of German).
- Give teams a brief learning game (e.g., Famous Presidents: (1) L _ _ C _ _ N, (2) R _ _ S _ V _ _ T, and so forth).

You can also use this time to give your students a demonstration of how an effective learning team functions. If you can, make a brief video that shows an effective learning team in action. Alternatively, invite a small group of students to role-play an effective team. During their role-playing demonstration, coach the group as they struggle to perform a team-learning task.

3. INVITE TEAMS TO DISCUSS GROUND RULES AND RESPONSIBILITIES.

Talking about ground rules helps long-term learning teams to concretize how they must function in order to reach their goals. You can ask teams to brainstorm potential ground rules or provide them with a checklist such as the following.

Our Ground Rules

The following are ground rules that are helpful to learning teams. Check those most important to you.

_____ Start on time with everyone present.

_____ Get to know members who are different from you.

_____ Let others finish without interrupting them.

_____ Be brief and to the point.

_____ Be prepared.

_____ Give everyone a chance to speak.

_____ Share the workload.

If long-term teams are going to be effective, some crucial jobs have to be done. If no one does them, the teams will drift aimlessly without achieving much. To make this point, you might want to share the following well-circulated story:

> *A team had four members called Everybody, Somebody, Anybody, and Nobody. There was an important job to be done. Everybody was sure that Somebody would do it. Anybody could have done it, but Nobody did it. Somebody got angry about that because it was Everybody's job. Everybody thought Anybody could do it, but Nobody realized that Everybody wouldn't do it. It ended up that Everybody blamed Somebody when Nobody did what Anybody could have done.*

Then ask teams to consider assigning themselves (preferably on a rotating basis) some of the following important jobs.

- *Facilitator:* Facilitates learning team sessions.
- *Timekeeper:* Allocates and monitors time needed and spent.
- *Secretary or note taker:* Keeps a record of ideas, conclusions, and achievements.
- *Checker:* Sees if all members are doing what they are supposed to.
- *Investigator:* Finds things out and brings information back to the team.

PLANNING SHEET

Build Learning Teams before Giving Students Work

Use the following sheet to implement this strategy.

Technique (check one or more):

_____ Utilize team-building activities.

_____ Give students a brief taste of team learning.

_____ Invite teams to discuss ground rules and responsibilities.

My Plan:

_____

_____

_____

_____

_____

_____

_____

_____

_____

_____

_____

_____

_____

_____

_____

_____

_____

_____

STRATEGY #19:
Gradually Immerse Students in Team Learning

Many teachers conduct their classes in traditional ways and then all of a sudden put students into groups and burden them with long-term, complex assignments and projects (e.g., a research or development project). Sometimes things go well, but all too often it's a disaster. That won't happen to you if you gradually immerse your students in team learning. Heed the advice presented in the following sections.

1. STRUCTURE THE FIRST LEARNING TASKS FOR SUCCESS.

Keep the first tasks short. An early round of 20- to 30-minute team-learning activities will get students used to the process and are less likely to bring out poor group dynamics. For example, you might ask students to do any of the following.

- Discuss a short case study and propose a solution.
- Read and clarify a one-paragraph text or a well-bulleted one-page handout.
- Complete a simple scientific experiment together.
- Compose a brief statement together.
- Translate a short dialogue or newspaper article.
- Answer a brief number of questions.
- Brainstorm a list of creative ideas.

It's also a good idea to provide enough background information so that your students can handle any of these tasks successfully. It's also helpful to have students do a task by themselves first and then together as a team. In addition, give students tasks that cannot be completed by simply dividing the work (i.e., can be done without any significant collaboration). The better tasks pool the resources of the group to complete them.

You also will promote early success if you are specific about your expectations. If you leave it up to students how to go about their work, they may not be ready yet to function well on their own. Therefore, it's a good idea to request a desired result. For example, don't just ask students merely to discuss a short text. Have them produce one question about the text. Don't just ask students to answer a set of questions verbally. Have them write out their answers.

Finally, it's important early on to monitor the quality of the team's work and to provide feedback. Review the learning tasks you initially give them so that students obtain a clear idea what a quality outcome looks like. Take the time to show them examples of successful work.

2. UP THE CHALLENGE LEVEL OF THE NEXT ROUND OF TEAM-LEARNING ACTIVITIES.

As your students become more accustomed to team learning, give them longer and more challenging assignments. However, keep your expectations quite specific. They are not yet ready to learn in teams without supervision. Hold them accountable for specific outcomes, such as a progress report, a completed project, and so forth. You might also decide to grade their work as a group.

At the same time, promote self-responsibility and group ownership by introducing the experience of *group processing*. Teams that go about their business without ever reflecting on how well they are doing eventually flounder. Ask learning teams to discuss their progress in order to build the type of awareness that keeps the team from going off the deep end. Point out that all teams have problems and that if these are not brought to the surface they won't go away. Use any of the following processes.

- *Helpful versus unhelpful:* What behaviors have we used thus far that are helpful? What behaviors are unhelpful?
- *In hindsight:* If we had a chance to do that over again, what would we do?
- *Right and wrong:* What's going right or wrong? What's going right in the team? What's going wrong?
- *Stop, start, continue:* What should we stop doing? Start doing? Continue doing?

Although learning teams still require supervision at this stage, begin to lessen the time you spend monitoring what's happening in teams. Leave students unobserved for stretches of time and even consider leaving the room as a sign that you trust their maturity to learn on their own.

3. EMPOWER EXPERIENCED LEARNING TEAMS TO WORK WITHOUT YOUR CLOSE SUPERVISION.

As learning teams become oriented to team learning and show signs of taking responsibility for their own learning, you can begin to give them tasks that are more demanding and less structured. For example, you might provide a list of questions that teams investigate through reading, interviewing, and observing between class sessions. The following are some questions given to learning teams in a class on human sexuality.

- Is there anything "normal" about human sexual activity?
- What constitutes a person's "sexual self-image"?
- What are the advantages and disadvantages of different methods of birth control?
- What sexually transmitted diseases are most common today? How are they transmitted and treated?

The teams are given a total of six hours to meet, both in and outside class, to investigate these questions. They are provided with plenty of resources to gather information but how they organize themselves and how they report their findings is largely left up to them. Another way of empowering the teams is to ask them to do some collaborative problem solving, as in the following example.

> *As a group, find out why the electoral college was created and how it is defended in the present political climate. Then, decide if it should be modified or eliminated. Create a presentation on your decision.*

Consider also giving learning teams the responsibility of preparing and teaching a lesson to the rest of the class. For example, in a course on creativity three teams were the given one of the following assignments.

- Teach others four different types of brainstorming techniques.
- Teach others about "reframing" and "perspective shifting."
- Teach others how to use "mind mapping" to create novel solutions.

Whenever you give teams a serious assignment or project, there is always the concern that students will not be equally hard working. One way to create both fairness and motivation is to base part of students' grades on peer evaluation. For example, you can ask students to apportion a designated number of points (e.g., 100) among its members in terms of each member's contribution to their team's assignment or project. (Students do not give points to themselves.)

PLANNING SHEET

Gradually Immerse Students in Team Learning

Use the following sheet to implement this strategy.

Technique (check one or more):

_____ Structure the first learning tasks for success.

_____ Up the challenge level of the next round of team-learning activities.

_____ Empower experienced learning teams to work without your close supervision.

My Plan:

_____

_____

_____

_____

_____

_____

_____

_____

_____

_____

_____

_____

_____

_____

_____

_____

_____

_____

_____

STRATEGY #20:
Use a Variety of Team-Learning Activities
....

A wide range of activities exists that you can give to learning teams. If you utilize some of those, you will find that your students will look forward to the experience of working in learning teams. Let's look at some options.

1. CREATE STUDY GROUPS.

Give teams some learning material and ask them to explain it to one another. This method gives students the responsibility of studying learning material and clarifying its content as a group without the teacher's presence. The assignment needs to be specific enough that the resulting study session will be effective and the group is able to be self-managing.

Procedure:

1. Give students a short, well-formatted handout covering lesson material, a brief text, or an interesting chart or diagram. Ask them to review it silently. The study group will work best when the material is moderately challenging or open to interpretation.

2. Form subgroups and give them a quiet space in which to conduct their study sessions.

3. Provide clear instructions that guide students to study and explicate the material carefully. Include directions such as the following.
   - *Clarify* the content.
   - *Create* examples, illustrations, or applications of the information or ideas.
   - *Identify* points that are confusing or with which you disagree.
   - *Argue* with the text; develop an opposing point of view.
   - *Assess* how well you understand the material.

4. Assign jobs such as facilitator, timekeeper, recorder, or spokesperson to subgroup members.

5. Reconvene the entire group and do one or more of the following.
   - Review the material together.
   - Quiz students.
   - Obtain questions.
   - Ask students to assess how well they understand the material.
   - Provide an application exercise for students to solve.

2. HAVE STUDENTS SEARCH FOR INFORMATION.

Give teams some questions and provide learning material that contains the answers. Have them find the answers. This method can be likened to an open-book test. Teams search for information (normally covered by the teacher) that answers questions posed to them. This method is especially helpful in livening up dry material.

Procedure:

1. Create a group of questions for which the answers can be found in resource material you have made available to students. Such material might include the following.
    - Handouts
    - Documents
    - Textbooks
    - Reference guides
    - Computer-accessed information
    - Artifacts
    - Equipment
2. Hand out the questions about the topic.
3. Form participants into small teams and have them search for the answers. A friendly competition can be set up to encourage participation.
4. Reconvene the group and review answers. Expand on the answers to enlarge the scope of learning.

3. PROMOTE GROUP POWER.

Let students experience that several heads are better than one. Give them a thought-provoking question to answer individually. They then share their answers with one another and produce a group answer.

Procedure:

1. Give students one or more questions that require reflection and thinking. The following are some examples:
    - How do our bodies digest food?
    - What is knowledge?
    - What is "due process"?
    - How is the human brain like a computer?
    - Why do bad things sometimes happen to good people?

2. Ask students to answer the questions individually.

3. After all students have completed their answers, create small groups and ask them to share their answers with each other in their respective groups.

4. Ask the groups to create a new answer to each question, improving on each individual's response.

5. When all groups have written new answers, compare the answers of each group in the class.

4. HOLD LEARNING TOURNAMENTS.

Give teams material to master in preparation for inter-team competition. This technique combines a study group with team competition. It can be used to promote the learning of a wide variety of facts, concepts, and even skills.

Procedure:

1. Divide students into teams of two to eight members. Make sure the teams have an equal number of members. (If this can't be done, you will have to average each team's score.)

2. Provide the teams with material to study together, such as lecture notes, a brief text, or an interesting chart or diagram.

3. Develop several questions that test comprehension of the learning material. Use formats that make self-scoring easy, such as multiple choice, fill-in-the-blanks, true/false, or terms to define.

4. Give a portion of the questions to students. Refer to this as Round 1 of the learning tournament. *Each participant must answer the questions individually.*

5. After the students have completed the questions, provide the answers and ask students to count the number of questions they answered correctly. Then, have them pool their scores with every other member of their team to obtain a team score. Announce the scores of each team.

6. Ask the teams to study again for the second round of the tournament. Then ask more questions as part of Round 2. Have teams once again pool their scores and add them to their Round 1 scores.

7. You can have as many rounds as you like, but be sure to allow the teams a study session between each round.

PLANNING SHEET

Use a Variety of Team-Learning Activities

Use the following sheet to implement this strategy.

Technique (check one or more):

_____ Create study groups.

_____ Have students search for information.

_____ Promote group power.

_____ Hold learning tournaments.

My Plan:

_____

_____

_____

_____

_____

_____

_____

_____

_____

_____

_____

_____

_____

_____

_____

_____

_____

_____

STRATEGY #21:
Invite Students to Teach Each Other

....

Aristotle declared: "Teaching is the highest art of understanding." When students are allowed to teach each other, both the students who teach and the students who learn benefit. The following are some ways of promoting peer teaching.

1. JIGSAW THE LEARNING.

Jigsaw learning is a creative form of peer teaching. It is an exciting alternative whenever there is material to be learned that can be segmented or "chunked" and when no single segment must be taught before the others. Each participant learns something that when combined with the material learned by others forms a coherent body of knowledge.

Choose learning material that can be broken into segments. A segment can be as short as one sentence or as long as several pages. (If the material is lengthy, ask students to read their assignments before the session.) Examples of appropriate material include the following.

- A multipoint handout
- A text that has different sections or subheadings
- A list of definitions
- A group of magazine articles or other types of short reading material

Count the number of learning segments and the number of students. In an equitable manner, give out different assignments to different subgroups. For example, imagine a class of 12 students. Assume that you can divide learning materials into three segments or "chunks." You might then be able to form quartets, assigning each group Segment 1, 2, or 3. Then ask each quartet or "study group" to read, discuss, and learn the material assigned to them. (If you wish, you can form pairs or "study buddies" first and then combine the pairs into quartets.)

After the study period, form "cooperative learning" subgroups. Such subgroups contain a representative from each study group in the class. In the example just given, the members of each quartet could count off 1, 2, 3, 4. Form cooperative learning subgroups of students who have the same number. The result will be four trios. In each trio will be one person who has studied Segment 1, one who has studied

Segment 2, one who has studied Segment 3, and one who has studied Segment 4. Ask the members of the cooperative learning subgroups to teach one another what they have learned. Alternatively, give these subgroups a set of questions, a problem to solve, or any other assignment that depends on the pooled knowledge of its members for completion. Reconvene the full class for review and answer remaining questions to ensure accurate understanding.

2. GIVE STUDENTS THE OPPORTUNITY TO ANSWER EACH OTHER'S QUESTIONS.

Hand out an index card to each student. Ask students to write down either a question they have about the learning material being studied in the class (e.g., a reading assignment) or a specific topic they would like discussed in class.

In a class on American short stories, for example, the teacher might set the foundation for class discussion on the story "The Lottery" (by Shirley Jackson) by distributing index cards and asking students to write down a question they have about the story. The following are examples of questions submitted by students and then redistributed to the class for response.

a. Who were the villagers attempting to please by holding the lottery?

b. How did the ritual of the lottery start?

c. Why didn't anyone stop the stoning?

d. Why was Mr. Summers in charge of the lottery?

Collect the cards, shuffle them, and distribute one to each student. Ask each student to read silently the question or topic on his or her card and think of a response. Invite a willing volunteer to read his or her card out loud and give a response. After a response is given, ask the others in the class to add to what the volunteer has contributed. Continue as long as there are volunteers.

3. HAVE A SMALL GROUP OF STUDENTS CONDUCT ENTIRE LESSONS.

Divide the class into subgroups. Create as many subgroups as you have topics to be taught. Give each group some information, a concept, or a skill to teach others. The following are example topics.

- The structure of an effective paragraph
- Psychological defense mechanisms
- Solving a math puzzle
- The spread of AIDS

Ask each group to design a way of presenting or teaching its topic to the rest of the class. Advise them to avoid lecturing or reading a report. Urge them to make the learning experience for students as active as possible. Make some of the following suggestions.

- Provide visual aids.
- Develop a demonstration skit (where appropriate).
- Use examples and/or analogies to make teaching points.
- Involve students through discussion, quiz games, writing tasks, role-play, mental imagery, or case study.
- Allow for questions.

For example, a teacher assigns a sociology class the task of developing classroom presentations on four major issues of *aging*. Four subgroups are formed that choose from among the following formats for peer teaching.

- *The aging process:* A true/false quiz game on facts of aging
- *Physical aspects of aging:* A simulation of typical aspects of aging (e.g., arthritis, decreased hearing, and blurred vision)
- *Stereotypes of aging:* A writing task in which class members write about society's perceptions of the elderly
- *Loss of independence:* A role-play exercise involving an adult child discussing issues of transition with his or her parent

Allow sufficient time for planning and preparation (either in or outside class). Then, have the groups present their lessons. Instead of group teaching, have students teach or tutor others individually or in small groups.

4. CREATE POSTER SESSIONS.

This alternative presentation method is an excellent way to inform briefly, capture the imagination, and invite an exchange of ideas among students. This technique is also a novel and graphic way of enabling students to express in a nonthreatening environment their perceptions and feelings about the topic you are currently discussing.

Ask every student to select a topic related to the general class topic or unit being discussed or studied. Request that students prepare a visual display of their concept on poster board, bulletin board, and so on (you will determine the size). The poster display should be self-explanatory; that is, observers would easily understand the idea without any further written or oral explanation. However, students may choose to prepare a one-page handout to accompany the poster that offers more detail and serves as further reference material.

During the designated class session, ask students to post their visual presentations and freely circulate around the room viewing and discussing each other's posters. A health class, for example, is studying about stress. Assigned topics include the following.

- Causes of stress
- Symptoms of stress
- Effects of stress on self and others
- Stress reducers

One of the students illustrates the symptoms of stress by creating a poster display that shows the following pictures.

- An overweight person on a scale
- Someone drinking an alcoholic drink
- Two people arguing
- A person with a headache

Below each picture is a short paragraph explaining how and why a stressed person might be exhibiting the symptom portrayed.

PLANNING SHEET

Invite Students to Teach Each Other

Use the following sheet to implement this strategy.

Technique (check one or more):

_____ Jigsaw the learning.

_____ Give students the opportunity to answer each other's questions.

_____ Have a small group of students conduct entire lessons.

_____ Create poster sessions.

My Plan:

_____

_____

_____

_____

_____

_____

_____

_____

_____

_____

_____

_____

_____

_____

_____

_____

....

Enhance Learning with Experiencing and Doing

Jean Piaget, the renowned developmental psychologist, taught us that children learn concretely but become capable of abstract thought as they enter adolescence. Unfortunately, many teachers have taken this change in mental capacity to mean that concrete learning experiences can now be curtailed.

Learning by experiencing and doing should continue throughout a person's lifetime. For example, students can understand the physics of bridges through constructing miniature models of bridges. They can understand the dynamics of the stock market through tracking an imaginary portfolio of equities. They can understand the problems faced by visually impaired people through participating in a simulation of blindness. The need for concrete experience doesn't diminish, but with the capacity for abstract thinking students can now go from the experience to much higher-order understandings.

Experiential learning not only enhances the understanding of concepts but serves as a gateway to skill development. Whenever you want students to develop skills (e.g., writing poetry, creating spreadsheets, operating a machine, or interviewing for a job), it's imperative to go beyond showing them how to do it. They must do it themselves, not just once but often—at first with your guidance and then on their own. Let's explore some key strategies for promoting learning by experiencing and doing.

STRATEGY #22:
Create Experiences That Simulate or Match Reality
....

The starting point of experiential learning is the actual experience in which you want to immerse your students. There are several challenges in their actual creation. The most notable are:

- Time may be limited.
- For practical reasons, you can't provide the "real thing."
- Students may be apprehensive.

The sections that follow explore tips that may help in this area.

1. JOLT YOUR STUDENTS WITH A BRIEF BUT SURPRISING EXPERIENCE.

Create quick dramatic activities that surprise students about something they normally take for granted or about which they hold untested assumptions. These "jolts" are great segues into serious conversations. Consider two ways of "jolting" students. One is to ask students to do something and then observe the result and discuss its implications. (For example, asking a student to cross his arms and then recross them the opposite way will seem uncomfortable even though about half the audience will find the "recross" to be perfectly comfortable.) A second way is to ask students to watch you say, show, or do something in which the result is unexpected. (For example, you can demonstrate the difficulties of using the English language by showing that a simple word such as *run* can be used to mean over 10 different actions.) After the jolt, invite students to react to it. Be careful not to act as if you are leading them to a predetermined insight or conclusion. Even if you feel that the jolt has a clear lesson or message, find out what your students think first. They may "jolt" you!

2. HAVE STUDENTS ACT IT OUT.

Sometimes, no matter how clear an explanation is or how descriptive visual aids are, certain concepts and procedures are not understood. One way to help clarify the material is to ask some students to act out the concepts or walk through the procedures you are trying to explain. Some examples include the following.

- The difference between a complete and an incomplete sentence
- Finding a common denominator

- Corporeal (heart) circulation
- Gothic architecture
- The construction of a database

Use any of the following methods to act something out.

- Invite some students to come to the front of the room, and have each physically simulate an aspect of the concept or procedure.
- Create large cards that name the parts of a procedure or concept. Distribute the cards to some students. Ask the students with cards to arrange themselves so that the steps of the procedure are correctly sequenced.
- Develop a role-play in which students dramatize the concept or procedure.
- Ask students to volunteer to demonstrate a procedure that involves several people.
- Build a model of a process or procedure.
- Have students physically manipulate components of a process or system.
- Videotape a group of people illustrating the concept or procedure and show it to the students.
- Ask students to create a way of acting out a concept or procedure without your guidance.

3. HAVE STUDENTS EXPERIENCE "BEING IN SOMEONE ELSE'S SHOES."

You can give your students an understanding and sensitivity to people or situations that are unfamiliar to them. One of the best ways of accomplishing this goal is to create an activity that simulates that unfamiliar person or situation. Begin by choosing a type of person or situation you want students to learn about. You may elect to have students experience what it is like to be any of the following.

- In the "minority"
- In a different age group
- From a different culture
- A person with special problems or challenges
- A person with a demanding job (e.g., a doctor)

Then, create a way of simulating that person or situation. Among the ways to do this are the following.

- Have students dress in the attire of that person or situation. Alternatively, have them handle the equipment, props, accessories, or other belongings of that person or situation or engage in a typical activity.
- Place students in situations in which they are required to respond in the role or character they have been given.
- Impersonate an individual and ask the students to interview you and find out about your experiences, views, and feelings.
- Use an analogy to build a simulation. Create a scenario familiar to students that sheds light on an unfamiliar situation. (You might, for instance, ask all students in your class who are left-handed to portray people who are culturally different from the rest of the students.)

An example of a simulation is Instant Aging. This simulation is designed to sensitize students to sensory deprivation and the normal process of aging. Students are given eyeglasses smeared with Vaseline, dried peas to put in their shoes, cotton for their ears, and latex gloves for their hands. Each student is then asked to take out a pencil and paper and write down his or her name, address, telephone number, any medication currently being taken, and any known allergies. Next, the students are told to take a walk outside the classroom, first opening the door and then finding their way around. The simulation involves further directions concerning the order of applying the props, the specific details of the tasks students are asked to perform, and how they are to take turns assisting each other.

Ask students how they felt during the simulation. Discuss the experience of being in someone else's shoes. Invite students to identify the challenges that unfamiliar persons and situations present to them.

4. ARRANGE FOR STUDENTS TO EXPERIENCE THE "REAL DEAL."

Have students experience something just as it is or as close to "the real deal" as possible. The following are examples.

- Going on a field trip that involves doing (not just observing)
- Conducting an experiment
- Producing a document
- Temporarily working alongside or replacing a person on a job
- Visiting an environment unfamiliar to students

PLANNING SHEET

Create Experiences That Simulate or Match Reality

Use the following sheet to implement this strategy.

Technique (check one or more):

_____ Jolt your students with a brief but surprising experience.

_____ Have students act it out.

_____ Have students experience "being in someone else's shoes."

_____ Arrange for students to experience the "real deal."

My Plan:

_____

_____

_____

_____

_____

_____

_____

_____

_____

_____

_____

_____

_____

_____

_____

_____

_____

_____

_____

STRATEGY #23:
Ask Students to Reflect on the Experience
....

Experience is not the "best teacher." Reflected experience is. Don't depend on the experience itself to lead to significant learning. Students can get so caught up in the experience that it remains unexamined and its meaning is lost. Students will get the most from any experience if you hold the following three discussions.

1. ASK STUDENTS TO DISCUSS WHAT HAPPENED TO THEM DURING THE EXPERIENCE.

Students can quickly forget what happened during an experience. The following are some questions to ask that help students recall what happened and that bring certain aspects of the experience into awareness.

- What did you do? (e.g., "What did you do during the experiment that was useful? a waste of time?")
- What did you observe? think about? (e.g., "What did you notice when 'left-handed' students were participating in the exercise?")
- What feelings did you have during the experience? (e.g., "Did you like being 'mayor for a day'?")

Use any of the discussion options suggested in Step 3 (on pages 49–52 of this book) to generate responses.

2. ASK STUDENTS TO THINK ABOUT WHAT LESSONS THE EXPERIENCE TAUGHT THEM.

Here is where their abstract thinking skills come into play. Have students make deductions from what happened, what they observed, and what they felt. Use reflection questions such as:

- What did you learn about _____? (e.g., "What makes a bridge sturdy?")
- What did you already know that you relearned from this experience? (e.g., From this exercise, what are some of the reasons people have stereotypes?)

- What benefits did you get from the experience? (e.g., How did the experience of assisting a blind person for one afternoon sensitize you to the problems blind people have and to the skills they must develop as compensation for their lack of sight?)

- If it is a simulation or role-play: How does the experience relate to the real world? (e.g., What can you conclude about the wisdom of how the Constitution is amended from the simulation you just went through?)

Make a list of the "lessons learned."

3. ASK STUDENTS IF THEY WANT TO DO ANYTHING DIFFERENTLY IN THE FUTURE.

This step is the application phase. Now that the experience is ended and it has been thoroughly analyzed, do your students want to do anything new or different? Ask them questions such as:

- What do you want to do differently next time? (e.g., when you meet a person whose English is difficult to understand)

- What else can we do about _____? (e.g., homeless people)

- How will this experience affect you when _____? (e.g., you return home or to work)

- What steps can you take to apply what you learned about _____? (e.g., mixing media)

You might want to ask students to write their answers to such questions, and then invite those who are willing to share their answers with others.

PLANNING SHEET

Ask Students to Reflect on the Experience

Use the following sheet to implement this strategy.

Technique (check one or more):

_____ Ask students to discuss what happened to them during the experience.

_____ Ask students to think about what lessons the experience taught them.

_____ Ask students if they want to do anything differently in the future.

My Plan:

_____

_____

_____

_____

_____

_____

_____

_____

_____

_____

_____

_____

_____

_____

_____

_____

_____

STRATEGY #24:
Avoid "Monkey See, Monkey Do"

Learning by doing is critical to developing skills. For example, your students can watch you demonstrate how to solve quadratic equations or how to order food in French, but unless they do it themselves they will not develop the skill and retain it over time.

Although most teachers agree with the proposition that students must do it themselves, they often encourage a form of doing that is more like imitation than anything that requires thinking. Let me explain why.

Some skills involve only a single step. For example, "dragging" over a paragraph on a computer screen allows you to select that text for a number of modifications (e.g., replacing, cutting, copying, and so forth). If a teacher shows students how to do that action and the student immediately repeats what the teacher does, the student is, in effect, imitating the teacher—or as I would put it, "seeing what the monkey is doing, and then doing it." Learning by imitation is very short-lived. Unless the student repeats the behavior over and over again, day in and day out, he or she will not automatically retain the skill, even if the skill is not difficult. What seems easy to do immediately after a brief demonstration is now lost among a myriad of other skills a student has been taught in the interim. The "monkey" is out of sight and, hence, "out of mind." Any teacher will recognize this moment whenever a student no longer remembers how to do something you just showed him or her a day ago. The student could perform the skill yesterday, but since then many mental events have occurred and what was once known is now lost. If the teacher shows the student once again what to do, the student may be able to do the skill correctly yet still not remember it for long.

Moreover, many skills require several steps. Learning how to attach a document to an e-mail is an example. It's not one action but several in sequence. Because the initial learning of a skill necessitates a step-by-step process, teachers often take students one step at a time until the action is completed. Once the sequence is complete, the student achieves the final result. But, again, for how long? What may have occurred is that the student can perform the skill if prompted step by step but cannot perform it if he or she has to do the entire sequence by himself or herself. The following are some suggestions for avoiding "monkey see, monkey do."

1. SHOW, BUT DON'T TELL.

The classic way of teaching a skill is to do a show-and-tell demonstration before asking students to try it themselves. A more "active" approach is to demonstrate a skill, but with little or no explanation. Instead of telling students what you are doing, ask them to observe carefully the demonstration and tell you what you did. This strategy encourages students to be mentally alert.

Decide on a skill you want students to learn. Ask the students to watch you perform the skill. Just do it, with little or no explanation or commentary about what and why you are doing what you do. (Telling the students what you are doing will lessen their mental alertness.) Give the students a visual glimpse of the "big picture" (or the entire skill if it involves several steps). Do not expect retention. At this point, you are merely establishing readiness for learning. Then, put the students into pairs. Demonstrate the first part of the skill, with little or no explanation or commentary. *Ask pairs to discuss with each other what they observed you doing.* Ask for a volunteer to explain what you did. If the students have difficulty following the procedure, demonstrate again. Acknowledge correct observations. Have the pairs practice with each other the first part of the skill. When it is mastered, proceed with a silent demonstration of the remaining steps, following each part with paired practice. At the end, have students perform the entire sequence from the beginning to end.

If you have the opportunity to teach one student a skill, you can also use the "show but don't tell" approach, but be sure to make the student comfortable by asking questions such as: "What did you see me do?" "What else did I do?" "Would you like me to show you again?"

2. UP THE CHALLENGE LEVEL.

When students can perform a skill on their own once with your assistance, challenge them to redo the skill all by themselves (from beginning to end if it involves more than one step). If you have given them any learning aid that shows them what to do, ask them to put the aid away and try the skill without it.

This is an ideal time to pair students as "practice partners." Invite students to demonstrate to their partner how to perform the skill in question. Using practice pairs, students are challenged without having to perform under the watchful eye of the teacher or the glare of a class of peers.

You can also invite students who can perform a skill to serve as peer tutors for students who are still struggling. Be sure that the tutor does not seek to show off rather than assist. Remind tutors that the students they are helping must be able to do the skill by themselves. Merely showing fellow students what to do or correcting their performance will not get the job done.

You might also up the challenge by pushing students to perform a skill after a period of time has intervened and the skill might be forgotten. For example, after helping students apply one grammatical rule, you might go on and help them learn several other rules. The challenge you can provide is to have them (without any reminders from you) use a rule they learned a while back.

PLANNING SHEET

Avoid "Monkey See, Monkey Do"
Use the following sheet to implement this strategy.

Technique (check one or more):

_____ Show, but don't tell.

_____ Up the challenge level.

My Plan:

_____

_____

_____

_____

_____

_____

_____

_____

_____

_____

_____

_____

_____

_____

_____

_____

_____

_____

_____

STRATEGY #25:
Use Role-Play to Develop Verbal Skills

Some of the skills you want students to develop require verbal expression. Examples include:

- Public speaking
- Debating
- Negotiating
- Counseling
- Selling
- Interviewing
- Active listening
- Helping

The best tool for developing these verbal skills is role-playing. Role-playing activities allow students to observe, practice, and get feedback. The problem is that students typically dislike role-playing. The number one reason is that it makes them uncomfortable. They fear being embarrassed in front of peers and teachers as they attempt to deal with the situation in which they are placed. The number two reason is that role-playing feels contrived or artificial to many students. It's simply not the same as a real-life situation. Because of these objections, it's very difficult to win them over to role-playing. Many students are content to watch but not perform. The following are some ways of overcoming these obstacles.

1. BEGIN BY HAVING STUDENTS COACH YOU IN A ROLE-PLAY.

Use a technique I call Nonthreatening Role-Playing. It reduces the threat of role-playing by placing the teacher in the lead role and involving the class in providing the responses and setting the scenario's direction. Create a role-play in which you will demonstrate desired behaviors, such as handling a person when they are angry. Inform the class that you will play the leading role in the role-play. The students' job is to help you deal with the situation. Obtain a student volunteer to role-play the other person in the situation (e.g., the angry person). Give that student an opening script to read to help him or her get into the role.

Start the role-play but stop at frequent intervals and ask the class to give you feedback and direction as the scenario progresses. Don't hesitate to ask students to provide specific "lines" for you to utilize. For example, at a specific point say: "What should I say next?" Listen to suggestions from the audience and try one of them out. Continue the role-play so that students increasingly coach you on how to handle the situation. This gives them skill practice while you do the actual role-playing for them.

2. MAKE ROLE-PLAYING SAFE BY DOING IT IN PAIRS.

Pair students and give them a role-playing scenario to act out together without public scrutiny. Arrange enough private space so that student pairs can role-play simultaneously. There is no guarantee that every pair will take the assignment seriously, but more will than will not. If you wish, create trios instead of pairs. Have one person serve as an observer as the other two students role-play. You can "round-robin" through the trio so that each student gets an opportunity to role-play twice and observe once. It is almost impossible to monitor and provide guidance to each pair or trio if role-playing is happening simultaneously, but at least students will be getting their feet wet. After simultaneous role-playing, you can invite students to perform in front of the entire class, now that they have had time to practice. At this time, you can act as a skill coach, giving pointers and demonstrating new behaviors.

3. USE SCRIPTS.

If you want a way of showing students effective skills while at the same time making them feel safe, give them scripts to read that contain successful ways of handling situations. At first, they can simply read the scripts, with different students playing different characters. (You can also have students read scripts in pairs.) As the students learn effective approaches, challenge them to put the scripts away and try the situation without them. Alternatively, invite students to write their own scripts.

4. INTRODUCE WHOLE-CLASS ROLE-PLAYING BY ROTATING PARTS.

Once students are on stage-front before their peers, the pressure builds. A way of easing students into this format is to rotate the actors rapidly. For example, assume you have a student who is asked to stand up to peer pressure. You might obtain one or two volunteers to portray the pressuring peers. They can remain in this role throughout the role-play. The person under pressure can be given one shot at responding, and then another student can take over for him or her. You can involve several students in this role-play, none of whom have to be "on stage" very long.

5. CHALLENGE STUDENTS TO PERFORM AND RECEIVE FEEDBACK.

The most threatening but challenging forum in which students can develop their verbal skills is to perform an entire scene by themselves and then be open to feedback about their performance. There are many ways to engage students in this challenge.

- Create subgroups of students and have them perform in a small, private, and (one can hope) supportive setting.

- If possible, allow students to select the time when they are sufficiently confident to perform before the class.

- Begin the feedback session by inviting the student to assess his or her own performance. Usually, a student will be aware of some deficiencies, and it's easier for him or her to say them rather than hear them from peers.

- Avoid wide-open student feedback. Ask students to comment on the positives first. Instead of asking for "negatives," ask for "suggestions" about how a person might improve. At all times, do what you need to do to protect a student's self-esteem.

PLANNING SHEET

Use Role-Play to Develop Verbal Skills

Use the following sheet to implement this strategy.

Technique (check one or more):

_____ Begin by having students coach you in a role-play.

_____ Make role-playing safe by doing it in pairs.

_____ Use scripts.

_____ Introduce whole-class role-playing by rotating parts.

_____ Challenge students to perform and receive feedback.

My Plan:

_____

_____

_____

_____

_____

_____

_____

_____

_____

_____

_____

_____

_____

_____

_____

_____

....

Blend in Technology Wisely

With widespread availability of personal computers and the Internet, a classroom does not have to be limited any longer to teacher-led lessons; single-method, single-paced instruction; and face-to-face interaction with classmates. Much more is possible. For example, students can learn math skills at their own pace and with a choice of learning aids by working with a multimedia tutorial program. A group of students can take virtual field trips to other countries and cultures utilizing a wide variety of online resources, including maps, photos, interactive activities, and video clips. Students can collaborate with other students throughout the world as they fly paper airplanes and learn about data collection and analysis.

Furthermore, technological tools makes it easier to engage students in high-level, active learning. Because they can find information faster and utilize software that enables them to do many things with it, students are able to engage in critical thinking, analysis, and application.

Like any other educational revolution, the advent of e-learning can be handled wisely or unwisely. Some computer-based lessons still turn students into passive learners and low-level thinkers. Others seek to entertain but not to educate. Still others isolate students from the support of other peers.

Regardless of your circumstances, how you blend in technology will determine whether or not active learning, as we have been exploring it throughout this book, will be sustained. Each teacher's situation is unique. Perhaps your classroom has a single computer. Perhaps a computer lab facility has limited availability for in-class use. Whatever your circumstances, it is hoped that the strategies in this chapter will be helpful to you in making educationally wise decisions.

STRATEGY #26:
Encourage Active Exploration

One of the most common educational uses of the Web is for student research. Students are given or find on their own web sites that give them useful information on a topic they are investigating. From research activities on the Web, students not only learn about specific topics but learn how to manage information, a vital skill for the twenty-first century. The following are some ways of making this research an active learning experience.

1. GUIDE STUDENT SEARCH FOR INFORMATIVE WEB SITES.

Students can waste a lot of time searching for reliable information. Left on their own, they may be lost in a blizzard of web sites, and when they discover some that may be helpful they may not be critical consumers of information they contain. You can help them by

- Identifying specialized educational search engines that have links to web sites that have been reviewed as educationally relevant
- Teaching students how to evaluate a web site for objectivity, accuracy, and so forth
- Creating a *start* page of selected links to direct students to sites you recommend or are recommended by other teachers
- Directing students to on-line reference sites for topics that can be found in encyclopedias, dictionaries, maps, or biographies

In addition, consider using web-based scavenger hunts to encourage students to explore various on-line resources and engage in fact-finding exercises in each web site they visit. By challenging students to locate specific information, a web-based scavenger hunt activity guides them to essential resources.

2. PROVIDE SEARCH TIPS.

Share (or invite experienced classmates to share) with students search tricks, such as using the following.

- The "find-in-text" command to locate key words and then reading that section of the text to find what you are looking for
- Simple key words for searching educational directories
- More than one search engine or directory
- Quote marks for phrases, * after root words, +, −, AND, OR, and NOT

3. UTILIZE WEBQUESTS.

Webquests are highly structured ways of carrying out research projects. As a result, they help students become creative researchers rather than simply "surfing" from one site to another. Students are given a task in which some or all of the information used by students is drawn from the Web. They are designed to use students' time well, focusing on *using* information rather than on *looking for* it. They also support analysis, synthesis, and evaluation. Answers or solutions are not predefined, and therefore must be discovered or created by students.

You can find numerous webquests on the Web. You can also create your own. Make note of what you like about existing webquests and then incorporate those ideas. According to Bernie Dodge, the originator of the webquest concept, there are six parts to an effective webquest.

1. *Introduction:* Orients students and captures their interest
2. *Task:* End product expected of students
3. *Process:* Strategies students should use to complete the task
4. *Resources:* Web sites students will use to complete the task
5. *Evaluation:* How the results of the activity will be measured
6. *Conclusion:* Summary of the activity and encouragement to reflect on its process and results

Some examples of webquest tasks include:

- Solving mysteries
- Creating an oral (with media) presentation
- Responding to a case-study problem
- Developing a mission statement
- Constructing something
- Conducting an experiment

For instance, a webquest called Theater: Yesterday and Always uses the Web to investigate the origins of performance elements and techniques in ancient theater, especially Greek and Roman stagecraft. Among other topics, students explore the aspects of stagecraft of the ancient theater that are still common to modern theater. They also learn about ancient performance formats (e.g., tragedy and comedy) that can be found in modern performances. Then, each student chooses one element to research and uses it as the basis of an oral presentation to the class.

PLANNING SHEET

Encourage Active Exploration

Use the following sheet to implement this strategy.

Technique (check one or more):

_____ Guide student search for informative web sites.

_____ Provide search tips.

_____ Utilize webquests.

My Plan:

_____

_____

_____

_____

_____

_____

_____

_____

_____

_____

_____

_____

_____

_____

_____

_____

_____

_____

_____

STRATEGY #27:
Use Technology to Supplement Classroom Instruction

The purpose of technology is to supplement classroom instruction, not replace it. The key issue is how this is accomplished. There are a number of options as to when to employ technology in the learning process. The following are some considerations.

1. USE PRESENTATION SLIDES BRIEFLY DURING YOUR FORMAL LESSONS.

During your formal lessons, you may be using presentation slides to provide visual backup. Too many teachers overdo the slides. Each slide contains too many points, and there are far too many of them overall. So, limit your slides. Paradoxically, your students will be more engaged if you give them less to absorb. Also, add interest to your slides by using graphics, animation, and (if possible) video.

One simple way of getting students thinking is to show a slide without comment. Instead, ask students to read it to themselves and perhaps clarify its content with a partner. You can also engage students by asking them to guess the next bullet in a buildup slide.

Don't limit slides to displaying content. You can create slides that present:

- Questions for discussion
- A brief problem to solve
- Key directions for an experiential exercise
- A quiz or game

2. EMPLOY COMPUTER-BASED TOOLS AS INSTRUCTIONAL ENHANCEMENTS.

Technology should act as a time-saver, not as a time-waster. There are endless ways of using technology to enhance your students' learning experience. The following are some examples of things students can do electronically.

- Follow the stock market on-line and create virtual portfolios.
- Complete computer-based homework assignments.
- Experience on-line tutoring of basic skills.
- Hold group discussion.
- Track the weather.
- Use virtual microscopes.
- Employ software to record and display the mathematical relationships of geometric objects.
- Edit and proof their writing.
- Take virtual field trips.
- Create class presentations with images, text, sound, and video.

3. REINFORCE CLASSROOM INSTRUCTION WITH COMPUTER ACTIVITY.

Don't view computer learning as an extracurricular activity. See it as a vital way of reinforcing classroom instruction. The following are some examples.

- A teacher wants her students to explore the topic "Feeding the Family: Balanced Diet/Balanced Budget." She gives her students information on nutrition and reviews math skills related to unit pricing. She then assigns small groups to purchase groceries for a week of balanced meals within a specific budget. The teams examine the database of an on-line shopping service to gather details about nutrition and prices. An electronic spreadsheet is then created so that students can organize, compare, and analyze information.
- A teacher instructs his students on the concept of fractions and their uses. This core instruction takes several class periods. He then assigns his students a computer-based lesson ("Who Wants Pizza?") that reinforces what they already know and teaches new things about fractions that the teacher did not cover.
- Students in a mechanical physics class are taught Newton's laws using traditional lecture methods. To make Newton's laws visible, students are given the task of simulating the motion of an elevator. Working in teams, they gather data about the elevator in their classroom building and make the necessary calculations.

4. USE CLASSROOM TIME TO MOTIVATE STUDENT INVOLVEMENT IN SUSTAINED COMPUTER ACTIVITY.

When you want students to achieve most of the learning outcomes via computer-based learning activities, it is critical to build interest and motivation first. The classroom is an ideal place for that. You can use classroom activity as a warm-up for computer-based learning. The following are two examples.

- A history teacher uses class time to develop his students' interest in the Reconstruction period that followed the Civil War. Students follow a route to freedom based on the actual journeys of runaway slaves during the second half of the nineteenth century. Decisions must be made along the route. As they relive the experiences of the Underground Railroad, students also learn the consequences of those choices.

- A social studies teacher has her students role-play a scene in which they pretend to purchase a home. Students are astounded by the purchase price. The dramatization leads students to be curious about the entire home-building process. They are engaged in a computer-based activity that simulates everything involved, from site selection to final sale. Players collect zoning requirements, loan limits, environmental concerns, and so forth in building and even selling a three-dimensional home.

PLANNING SHEET

Use Technology to Supplement Classroom Instruction
Use the following sheet to implement this strategy.

Technique (check one or more):

_____ Use presentation slides briefly during your formal lessons.

_____ Employ computer-based tools as instructional enhancements.

_____ Reinforce classroom instruction with computer activity.

_____ Use classroom time to motivate student involvement in sustained computer activity.

My Plan:

_____

_____

_____

_____

_____

_____

_____

_____

_____

_____

_____

_____

_____

_____

_____

_____

_____

STRATEGY #28:
Promote Collaboration through Technology
··

Computer-based learning tools and resources allow students to be treated as individuals—to have highly customized learning experiences based on their background, individual talents and interests, age level, cognitive style, and so on. In addition to working alone, however, computer-based learning can promote student-to-student interaction. Students can work in a small group or as an entire class.

Student motivation is enhanced in projects that require on-line collaboration. Students can collaborate with fellow classmates and with students in nearby schools, and can participate in projects that invite students from all over the world to participate.

1. USE TECHNOLOGY TO HELP STUDENTS LEARN FROM EACH OTHER.

Step 5 explored a number of ways of promoting peer learning and peer teaching. Computers help students do this in special ways. The following are some examples.

- Students research on the Web how the constitutional principle of equal protection under the law has been interpreted in five cases. The students are each assigned one of the cases. Students are then placed in "jigsaw groups" in which each member has learned about each of the cases. The groups are given a new case involving the equal protection clause and asked to predict how the court might rule.

- Students are assigned the web sites of opposing candidates in a political campaign. They evaluate the ads, speeches, and campaign platforms of their assigned candidate. In mixed groups, they explain the issues and the positions taken by each candidate.

- Students learn about saltwater fish. The teacher creates teams, asking each to prepare a presentation on a fish of their choice. The presentation requires covering how the fish breathe, how they propel themselves in the water, how they reproduce, and what they eat. Each team creates a home page with hot links for each of the topics.

2. INVOLVE YOUR STUDENTS IN COLLABORATIVE ACTIVITY BEYOND THEIR OWN CLASSROOM AND SCHOOL.

There are many ways of sharing information, ideas, solutions, preferences, displays, and reports with students in other schools and with the greater community. Students can create on-line book reports, science demonstrations, discussion forums, and web sites. The following are some examples.

- Students adopt a nearby pond, learn about pond ecology, and make a presentation to the town commissioners on cleanup measures the pond may require.
- Students in different schools in one state read the same book and post journal reflections.
- Students in a dozen countries share information on their communities, including holidays, national symbols, famous countrymen, natural resources, and products.

3. PROMOTE COMPUTER-BASED LEARNING BY TEAMING WITH OTHER TEACHERS.

One of the ways to share the time, resources, and expertise needed to support good computer-assisted learning is to collaborate with other teachers in your school. The following is an account of how this happened in an urban high school.

A business education teacher, a biology teacher, and the school librarian created a unit on cell biology and cancer. The biology teacher taught students about the basics of the cell, the business education teacher taught the students about creating PowerPoint presentations, and the librarian helped with the on-line and library research the students needed to do. They did this with one group of students in the block schedule they shared with another group of students. The students gave their presentations to the other group. Realizing how much their peers had learned and how much they enjoyed the process, the students who were left out demanded that they have a similar opportunity!

PLANNING SHEET

Promote Collaboration through Technology

Use the following sheet to implement this strategy.

Technique (check one or more):

_____ Use technology to help students learn from each other.

_____ Involve your students in collaborative activity beyond their own classroom and school.

_____ Promote computer-based learning by teaming with other teachers.

My Plan:

_____

_____

_____

_____

_____

_____

_____

_____

_____

_____

_____

_____

_____

_____

_____

_____

_____

STEP EIGHT

....

Make the End Unforgettable

Many units or entire courses run out of steam at the end. In some cases, students are marking time until the close is near. In other cases, teachers are valiantly trying before time runs out to cover what they haven't gotten to. How unfortunate! What happens at the end needs to be "unforgettable." You want students to remember what they've learned. You also want students to feel that what they learned has been special. When you are preparing to end a unit or entire course, there are four areas to consider.

- How will students review what you have taught them?
- How will students assess what they have learned?
- How will students consider what to do about what they have learned?
- How will students celebrate their accomplishments?

Let's explore ways of accomplishing these goals.

STRATEGY #29:
Get Students to Review What's Been Learned

Reviewing is a valuable learning activity and can take many forms—from fun games to challenging assignments. The following are some tips.

1. UTILIZE THE FORMAT OF A TELEVISION QUIZ PROGRAM.

Adapt a TV quiz program such as *Jeopardy*, *Who Wants to Be a Millionaire?*, or *Wheel of Fortune*. It is not necessary to follow the show's format rigidly. Make accommodations that serve your needs. For example, *Who Wants to Be a Millionaire?* is basically a series of multiple-choice questions, graduated in difficulty. It is played by one contestant until that person fails to answer a question or quits the game. In a classroom situation, you could do the following.

1. Prepare a set of multiple-choice questions on your material that ranges from easy to very difficult. You can use any number of questions, as long as the most difficult one is awarded $1 million if answered correctly. For example, you might have fourteen questions, designated as $100, $200, $300, $500, $1,000, $2,000, $4,000, $8,000, $16,000, $32,000, $64,000, $250,000, $500,000, and $1,000,000 in value.

2. Divide your students into teams of three or four members and have each team select a captain.

3. Give teams a number, beginning with 1.

4. *Explain the following rules:* Team 1 will be asked the easiest question. The team is allowed only 10 seconds to answer. The "final answer" must be stated by the team captain. If he or she is correct, his or her team is awarded the designated amount (e.g., $100). The next team, in numerical order, will then be asked the next question (in order of difficulty) and will be awarded its designated amount (e.g., $200) if correct. When every team has had a turn answering a question, the game returns to Team 1. If at any time a team answers incorrectly, the captain from any of the remaining teams that stands up first can win bonus points for his or her team by providing the correct answer.

5. For the most difficult questions, a team can be given up to one minute to present their "final answer."

6. For the million-dollar question, have each team submit its answer on a card. Every team that gets it right will receive the ultimate reward.

7. Conduct the review game. After each question is successfully answered, elaborate on the question's significance to the group's learning goals.

8. Request each team to report their total winnings.

2. CREATE A REVIEW ACTIVITY BASED ON A POPULAR GAME.

You can also adapt the format of a popular game as the basis for class review. The following are some possibilities.

- *Crossword puzzles:* Construct a simple crossword puzzle. Create clues for the horizontal and vertical items using definitions, categories, examples, opposites, fill-in-the-blanks, and so forth.

- *Cards:* Use the format of any card game—such as *Poker, Go Fish, Solitaire,* and *Crazy Eights*—to engage students. Students can obtain desirable cards by giving correct answers, ideas, or solutions to problems. Card games can also be used to classify things (e.g., fats, carbs, and proteins) or to enumerate the order of things (e.g., the sequence used to renew your computer's desktop).

- *Anagrams:* Have students form a word or phrase by rearranging the letters of another word or phrase (e.g., *trenur no estinment* to *return on investment*).

- *Baseball:* Create questions that are worth singles, doubles, triples, and home runs. Have teams create a lineup of students. Consider the possibility of each team "pitching" its own questions to the opposing team.

- *Scrabble:* Invite students to form words related to your subject matter. You can have them select letters from an actual Scrabble game, or you can provide a word or phrase in which they must use each of its letters to create a new word or phrase.

- *Pictionary:* Create small groups and have one participant begin. The starting "picturist" selects a word card from a deck of words (e.g., key softword concepts or functions) and has five seconds to examine the word to be played. The timer is then turned and the picturist begins sketching picture clues for the team. The picturist may not use verbal or physical communication to teammates during the round. Sketching and guessing continue until the word is identified or time is up.

- *Football:* Create questions to obtain "first downs, field goals, and touchdowns" (with "extra points"). The team on "defense" can select or devise the questions the team on "offense" must answer in order to move down the field and score points.

- *Dice:* Roll one die to determine questions to be answered (graded in difficulty from 1 to 6) or to specify the quantity of ideas or answers a team must provide (e.g., six strategies to do web searches). Roll two dice to determine how many spots a team can advance toward a goal after completing a task or answering a question.

- *Darts:* Create questions that have different point values. Invite students to throw darts to obtain the opportunity to answer these questions.

- *Bingo/Tic-Tac-Toe:* There are many possibilities here, from a name game in which a student's name is selected from a hat to a quiz game in which answers are provided on a game sheet. In the latter case, students get the opportunity to "cover" answers by supplying the question they respond to.

3. USE A JIGSAW DESIGN TO CREATE A COMPREHENSIVE REVIEW.

When you want to challenge your students, you can create a more comprehensive activity. One of my favorites involves the use of a jigsaw.

- Devise a list of questions, problems, key concepts, and so forth that apply to the entire unit or course you want students to review. For example, you might list 20 questions that cover a unit on the U.S. Constitution.

- Create subgroups of students and assign each subgroup a part of the list. For example, you can create four groups of five students, each of whom receives five questions from the list of 20 questions on the Constitution.

- Ask each subgroup to answer the questions, solve the problems, or define the concepts assigned to it. (Decide if you want your students to do this process with or without using reference material.)

- Redistribute each subgroup so that there is at least one representative from each of the original groups in the subgroups (called "jigsaw groups") you have just created. For example, if there were four groups of five students assigned to a portion of the 20 questions on the Constitution, have each of those groups count off from one to five. This creates five groups of four students. In each of the five groups will be one student who has worked on the answers to 25 percent of the questions. By sharing the answers with each other, the entire list of 20 questions will be reviewed.

4. INVITE STUDENTS TO SUMMARIZE THE ENTIRE UNIT OR COURSE.

Explain to students that providing a summary of what you have taught would be contrary to the principle of active learning. Instead, tell them to summarize for themselves the unit or course. Divide students into subgroups of two to four members. Ask each subgroup to create its own summary. Encourage the subgroups to create an outline, a mind map, or any other device that will enable them to communicate the summary to others. Use any of the following questions to guide the students.

- What were the major topics we examined?
- What have been some of the key points?
- What experiences have you had in this unit/course? What did you get out of them?
- What ideas and suggestions are you taking away from this unit/ course?

Invite the subgroups to share their summaries.

5. ASK STUDENTS TO PERFORM A VARIETY OF SKILLS.

If you have been teaching students skills that can be performed, challenge them to a performance review. The following are some examples.

- Students display their Spanish-speaking skills in a series of skits.
- Students are given a research problem that requires using all of the Web search skills they have been taught.
- Students are asked to perform in a role-play that incorporates all of the interview skills they have practiced.
- Students are given a motor to repair that involves several skills they have acquired.

Give students time to prepare for their performance, or challenge them to perform without prior preparation. Even if students feel some pressure, try to relax them by labeling the performance their "pre-Broadway" show, final rehearsal, or practice recital. Encourage students to applaud each other's performances.

PLANNING SHEET

Get Students to Review What's Been Learned

Use the following sheet to implement this strategy.

Technique (check one or more):

_____ Utilize the format of a television quiz program.

_____ Create a review activity based on a popular game.

_____ Use a jigsaw design to create a comprehensive review.

_____ Invite students to summarize the entire unit or course.

_____ Ask students to perform a variety of skills.

My Plan:

_____

_____

_____

_____

_____

_____

_____

_____

_____

_____

_____

_____

_____

_____

_____

_____

_____

STRATEGY #30:
Ask Students to Evaluate Their Accomplishments

The end of a unit or course of study is a time for reflection. What have I learned? What do I now believe? What are my skills? What do I need to improve?

Allowing time for self-assessment gives students the opportunity to examine what the unit or course has meant to them. The suggestions that follow are structured ways of promoting this type of self-assessment.

1. HAVE STUDENTS RATE THEMSELVES.

Prepare a survey in which students rate themselves on items that reflect the learning they have acquired. You can ask them to evaluate such things as:

- The skills they have mastered (e.g., how well they can write)
- The information they've acquired (e.g., how informed they are about the body's immune system)
- The concepts they have understood (e.g., how well they understand the concept of multilinear causality)
- New or expanded areas of interest (e.g., how interested they are in doing research)

Make the survey user friendly by using simple devices such as the following.

- Checklist (e.g., "Check the skill areas below in which you have improved")
- Rating scale (e.g., "Rate your understanding of each concept: poor, fair, good, excellent")
- Sentence completion (e.g., "One topic I think about a lot is _____.")
- Short answer (e.g., "What's the topic about which you've increased your knowledge the most?")

It's important that students are honest with themselves. They will be if you make the survey something they complete only for themselves. At the same time, consider having students share those responses they want to reveal with a partner or in a small group of students.

2. HAVE STUDENTS IDENTIFY WHAT THEY HAVE LEARNED.

By the end of a unit or course, after much time has elapsed, your students' awareness of what they've learned may be low. You can counteract that by asking your students to take the time to consider what they are taking away from the class. These may include any of the following.

- New knowledge
- New skill
- Improvement in _____ (e.g., reading comprehension)
- Confidence in _____ (e.g., public speaking)

A fun way of doing this is to create small groups and invite them to place their own entries on a list titled "What We Are Taking Away." Have each group display its list. Ask students to walk by each list and invite each person to place a check mark next to learnings on the lists (other than on his or her own) that he or she is also taking away.

Survey the results, noting the most popular learnings. Also, mention any that are unusual and unexpected.

3. INVITE STUDENTS TO ASSESS HOW THEY HAVE CHANGED.

One of the most effective ways of designing a unit or course of study is to have students compare their views about the class topic at the beginning and to reassess these views at the end. You can help your students do this by asking them at the start of a unit or course questions such as:

- What makes a _____ effective (e.g., term paper)?
- What is the value of _____ (e.g., checks and balances)?
- What advice they would give themselves to be _____ (e.g., better computer programmers)?
- What solutions might they devise in dealing with a problem you pose (e.g., how to keep economic growth in check)?

Use any of the following formats.

- Group discussion
- Questionnaire
- Debate
- Written statement

At the end of a unit or course of study, ask students to express their views once again. Ask students whether their views have remained the same or have shifted. Discuss the factors that created shifts in viewpoints.

Another approach is to ask students to assess what they have gained from the class. It places them in the position of someone who "owns" their own learning expectations rather than someone who merely goes along for the ride. Ask students at the beginning of a class to write down what they hope to get out of the class. The following are some ways of structuring this exercise.

- Ask students to list their own learning goals for the class.
- Ask students to list what they have previously found difficult or uninteresting about the subject matter.
- Ask students to list ways in which they might be able to use what they will learn.

Set aside some time periodically to allow students to read their initial statement and consider what value the class has had for them thus far. At the end of the term, semester, or course of study ask students to assess whether their investment of time and effort in the class has been worthwhile in light of their initial hopes. Obtain feedback from students.

PLANNING SHEET

Ask Students to Evaluate Their Accomplishments

Use the following sheet to implement this strategy.

Technique (check one or more):

_____ Have students rate themselves.

_____ Have students identify what they have learned.

_____ Invite students to assess how they have changed.

My Plan:

_____

_____

_____

_____

_____

_____

_____

_____

_____

_____

_____

_____

_____

_____

_____

_____

STRATEGY #31:
Have Students Plan for the Future
....

At the conclusion of any class that has featured active learning, students will naturally ask, "Now what?" The success of active learning is really measured by how that question is answered; that is, how what has been learned in the class affects what students will do in the future. The suggestions that follow are designed to promote future planning. Some are fairly quick techniques you can use when time is limited. Others require more time and commitment but lead to even better results.

1. INVITE STUDENTS TO CONSIDER HOW TO CONTINUE LEARNING ON THEIR OWN.

Point out your hope that your students' learning not stop simply because the class is over. Suggest to students that there are many ways for them to continue learning on their own. Indicate that one way to do this is to brainstorm their own list of ideas to "keep on learning."

Create subgroups. Have each subgroup brainstorm ideas. The following are some all-purpose suggestions.

- Look for subject-related articles in newspapers, magazines, and so forth.
- Take another course in the same subject area.
- Create a future reading list.
- Reread books and review notes taken in class.
- Teach something you've learned to someone else.
- Get a job or take an assignment that uses the skills you have learned.

Reconvene the class and ask each subgroup to share their best ideas. (If you feel that this process would be too difficult for your students to do on their own, you can prepare in advance a list of suggestions for the students. Ask them to check those they feel would be suitable for them.)

2. ASK STUDENTS TO GIVE THEMSELVES LEARNING REMINDERS.

You can have students create reminders to use what they have learned. They can even place these reminders on signs they can attach to any surface (refrigerator, door, desk, and so on). Invite students to think about one or more of the following.

- One thing they have learned in the class ("Observation is the basis for all science.")

- A key thought or piece of advice they will keep in mind to guide them in the future ("Use topic sentences.")

- An action step they will take in the future ("Preview what you read before you read it.")

- A question to ponder ("What is my goal?")

Urge students to express themselves as concisely as possible. Have them brainstorm possibilities before making their selections. Encourage them to obtain reactions to their ideas from others. They might want to base their signs on well-known car bumper stickers such as "Honk if you _____" or on advertising slogans such as "_____. No book can match it."

Give out index cards and have students write down reminders. Gather the cards and pass them around the group. Have each student select three ideas from other members of the class that will serve them well.

3. ENCOURAGE STUDENTS TO CREATE A PLAN OF ACTION.

Your students might be more likely to follow up the learning experiences they have had with concrete actions if you invite them to make a contract with themselves. One simple approach is to ask students to write themselves a letter indicating what they are taking away from the class, as well as what steps they intend to take to use what they have learned or to continue to learn more about the subject on their own. Suggest that they could begin the letter with the words "I hereby resolve." Inform them that the letter is confidential. Ask them to place it in an envelope, address it to themselves, and seal the envelope. You can promise to mail the envelope at a later point. Alternatively, invite students to write you an e-mail containing their intentions. You can reply at a later point with a copy of their message and a friendly note: "How is everything going?"

Another approach is to ask students at the end of the class to fill out a follow-up form containing statements as to how they plan to apply what they have learned or how they will continue learning more about the subject. The following is a sample form.

FUTURE PLANNING FORM

Describe how you plan to apply this course and tell when and how you plan to apply it. Be specific.

A. Situation: _____

_____

    My plan to apply: _____

_____

_____

B. Situation: _____

_____

    My plan to apply: _____

_____

_____

Describe what you want to do to continue learning about _____ [insert subject].

_____

_____

_____

_____

_____

_____

_____

_____

_____

_____

_____

_____

When the form is completed, inform the students that their future planning sheet will be sent to them in three to four weeks. At that time, they are sent these follow-up instructions.

Please review your future planning sheet. Place the letter A next to those plans you have been able to apply successfully. Place the letter B next to those plans on which you are still working. Place the letter C next to those plans you have not been able to do anything about. Explain what obstacles prevented your application.

PLANNING SHEET

Have Students Plan for the Future

Use the following sheet to implement this strategy.

Technique (check one or more):

_____ Invite students to consider how to continue learning on their own.

_____ Ask students to give themselves learning reminders.

_____ Encourage students to create a plan of action.

My Plan:

_____

_____

_____

_____

_____

_____

_____

_____

_____

_____

_____

_____

_____

_____

_____

_____

_____

_____

STRATEGY #32:
Let Students Celebrate the End

Students should feel in a celebratory mood when they have completed the end of a unit or entire course of study. They have worked hard and accomplished a lot together. There are a variety of ways of marking the end.

1. HAVE STUDENTS REMINISCE ABOUT THE LEARNING ACTIVITIES THEY HAVE EXPERIENCED.

Reminiscing enables students to join together at the end of a class and celebrate what they have experienced. A fun way to achieve this is to create a large display of the title of the unit or course or subject matter. Merge the words in the title if there are more than one. For example, "ancient history" becomes *ancienthistory*. Give students marking pens. Explain how words can be created in *Scrabble* fashion, using the displayed title as a base. Review the information that words can be created:

- Horizontally or vertically
- Beginning with, ending with, and incorporating any available letters

Remind students, however, that two words cannot merge with each other. There must be a space between them. Permit proper names as words. Set a time limit and invite students to create as many key words as they can that are associated with the subject matter or the learning experiences that have taken place. Suggest that they divide the labor so that some students are recording while others are searching for new words. Call time, and have students count the words. Applaud the results! If the group size is unwieldy for this activity, divide the class into subgroups so that each can create a *Scrabble* board. Display the results together and tally the *total* number of words produced by the entire class. You can also simplify the activity by writing the course title or subject matter vertically and asking students to write (horizontally) a verb, adjective, or noun they associate with the title and that begins with each letter.

Another way of reminiscing is to give students a blank sheet of paper and tell them that it is time for their "final exam." Keep them in suspense about the exam. Tell them that their task is to write down, in order, the topics or learning activities they have experienced in the class. (At this point, reveal that this is a fun challenge that will not be graded.) After each student has finished (or given up!), generate a classwide list. Make adjustments until a correct list is obtained. With the list in view, ask students to reminisce about these experiences, recalling moments of fun, cooperation, and insight. Facilitate the discussion so that the exchange of memories brings a strong emotional closure to the class.

If you wish, provide a list of the topics or activities for students. Start the reminiscing discussion immediately. Rather than focusing on activities, focus the exercise on *moments to remember*. Leave this phrase open to interpretation. This may create a laughter-filled and perhaps nostalgic review of the class.

2. CONGRATULATE STUDENTS ON THEIR ACCOMPLISHMENTS.

The unit or course of study you have completed may have involved a great deal of student effort and success. The end is a time for giving recognition for a job well done. The following are some ways of expressing congratulations.

- Provide a certificate of achievement for each student.
- Have students line up and give the person in front of them a pat on the back or a high five.
- Have students create cards that express appreciation and gratitude for each other's teamwork.
- Create a giant mural that lists the class's accomplishments, both in words and in visual symbols.
- Treat the class to pizza, ice cream, or some other popular food.
- Devise a musical tribute to students (e.g., use the theme song "We Are the Champions").

3. GIVE STUDENTS AN OPPORTUNITY TO SAY "GOOD-BYE."

In many classes, students develop feelings of closeness toward other classmates. This is especially true if the students have taken part in active learning activities. They need to say good-bye to each other and express their appreciation for the support and encouragement given each other during the class. There are many ways of facilitating these final sentiments. The following are my favorites.

Use a skein of yard to connect students literally and symbolically. Ask everyone to stand and form a circle. Start the process by stating briefly what you have experienced as a result of facilitating the class. Holding the end of the yarn, toss the skein to a student on the other side of the circle. Ask that person to state briefly what they have experienced as a result of participating in the class. Then ask that person to hold the yarn and toss the skein to another student.

Have each student take a turn at receiving the skein, sharing reflections, and tossing the yarn on, continuing to hold onto their piece. The resulting visual is a web of yarn connecting every member of the group. Some of the comments that might be expressed include the following.

- "I'm glad I got to know people on a personal level."
- "I feel that I can be open and honest with everyone here."
- "I had fun in this class."
- "I'm going to think of ways to practice what I learned here."
- "You have been a great group!"

Complete the activity by stating that the class began as a collection of individuals willing to connect and learn from each other. Cut the yarn with scissors so that each person, though departing as an individual, takes a piece of the other students. Thank students for their interest, ideas, time, and effort.

My other favorite is to assemble students for a class photograph. It's best to create at least three rows: one row sitting on the floor, one row sitting in chairs, and one row standing behind the chairs. As you are about to take their picture, express your own final sentiments. Stress how much active learning depends on the support and involvement of students. Thank students for playing such a large part in the success of the class. Then, invite one student at a time to leave the group and become the "photographer." (Optional: Have each participant merely come up and view what a final picture of the class would look like.)

If the class is not too large, ask each student to share his or her final thoughts with the group. Ask the group to applaud the student for his or her contributions to the group. Promise to send the class picture to students. With a digital camera, all you need is an e-mail address! Your students can receive their memento right away.

PLANNING SHEET

Let Students Celebrate the End

Use the following sheet to implement this strategy.

Technique (check one or more):

_____ Have students reminisce about the learning activities they have experienced.

_____ Congratulate students on their accomplishments.

_____ Give students an opportunity to say "good-bye."

My Plan:

_____

_____

_____

_____

_____

_____

_____

_____

_____

_____

_____

_____

_____

_____

_____

_____

_____

_____

_____

Final Advice

At the beginning of this book, I promised to share with you eight steps for sparking active learning in your classroom. To review, these eight steps are as follows.

STEP ONE:	**Engage Your Students from the Start.**
STEP TWO:	**Be a Brain-Friendly Teacher.**
STEP THREE:	**Encourage Lively and Focused Discussion.**
STEP FOUR:	**Urge Students to Ask Questions.**
STEP FIVE:	**Let Your Students Learn from Each Other.**
STEP SIX:	**Enhance Learning with Experiencing and Doing.**
STEP SEVEN:	**Blend in Technology Wisely.**
STEP EIGHT:	**Make the End Unforgettable.**

I hope you are inspired to apply these teaching strategies with your students. I recognize, however, that inspiration doesn't ensure action. So, I would like to end with some final advice on incorporating the eight steps.

Throughout this book, I have highlighted the theme that you can make a difference in your classroom if you take the eight steps to heart. You have the opportunity to rise above the usual norms prevalent in too many schools today. Far too often, teachers tolerate practices in themselves and in others that shut down rather than open up student learning. By applying the strategies I have provided in this book, there is a strong likelihood your students will become the active learners who are needed in a rapidly changing world.

You can make a difference if you are willing to:

- Want it
- Learn it
- Try it
- Live it

Wanting It

Ask yourself if you are truly happy with the current state of student learning in your classroom. Do you want to accept the status quo, with students passive and their learning short lived? It would be great if there were a magic wand that would dust (or inoculate) every one of us with the courage to take the risks necessary to rise above the norm. But it doesn't exist. Are you willing to show some courage?

Learning It

It's one thing to be motivated to take action. It's another matter to do so intelligently. I hope you have learned or relearned some useful ideas from this book. You'll also find many other sources of teaching wisdom in a good bookstore or on-line. Exposing yourself to new approaches is necessary for your development as a teacher who brings out the best in students.

Trying It

We are often reluctant to change our habits because we don't know what will happen if we do. View your attempts to apply the strategies in this book as a "personal experiment in change." Choose one strategy at a time and stay with it for a week. Try it on for size and see if it fits you. Don't be afraid to tell your students that you are experimenting and want their feedback. Such a move gives you permission to use a new idea and invites them to be your partner in finding approaches that work.

Living It

If any of your experiments in change bring success, you're likely to continue practicing them for a while. However, the bumps and bruises of life intervene, and we are all prone to relapse. Recognize those barriers that get the best of your resolve, and think about what you need to do to overcome them. Maybe you need to obtain some support from others. Maybe you need to go back to what got you motivated in the first place to start the journey of change. They say, "Nobody likes a change except a wet baby!" Prove them wrong.

Enjoy your journey in teaching actively.

Index